The Deity of Christ Declared

A Primer from the Word of God

Dr. Peter L. Banfe, PhD, MMin, MSci, MBA

3rd Edition, 2021

Printed in the United States of America

ISBN: 979-8-9851624-0-0

www.MissiontoBurma.com

Contents

Introduction

In this primer on the deity of Christ, it is this author's intention to lay out before the reader an indisputable case for the deity of Our Lord Jesus Christ. The overriding weight of the evidence proposed within this primer derives from the biblical record. However, a rich collection of early church documents expressing the overwhelming consensus of the early church fathers regarding the deity of Christ is also used as evidence of the fundamental belief that Christ is God.

This primer begins with the basic assumption that the Bible is the "absolute, supreme, authoritative, infallible, and unchangeable standard for faith and practice" (Watts, 1998). The foundational assumption is that the Bible is the revelation of God to man, put into words by men divinely inspired by the Creator to reveal His truth to us, divinely preserved. It is the Book of God. Therefore, this primer is largely a journey through Scripture to identify the Revelation of God as regarding His Son, Jesus Christ our Lord as the incarnate God.

There is no truth more fundamental to our faith than that of the deity of Christ. If He were not God, Calvary would have no power and our faith would be in vain. We would still be dead in our sins and would have no hope, no promise. We would have only an empty covenant that was never sealed by the blood of the atoning sacrifice of the only acceptable sinless Sacrifice, our Lord Jesus Christ, the One True God. There are seven separate streams of evidence presented to support an indisputable case for the deity of Christ.

This primer shows the weight of Scripture bearing testimony to Christ as God, including:

- Straightforward claims of His deity
- Messianic prophesy supporting the divine origin of Jesus
- All of the divine names and titles applied to Him to guide and direct people clearly to the conclusion that He is deity
- What He indicated about Himself by His words and the Bible's clear testimony
- The divine attributes He shares with God as the second person of the Holy Trinity
- The indisputable light His sinless, holy, supernatural life, death, burial, resurrection, ascension, and return brought to bear on His deity

This author's prayer is that the testimony of this primer on the deity of Christ might encourage everyone to bow in honor and worship the Word who "was God" (John 1:1), "my Lord and My God" (John 20:28), the "God with us" (Matthew 1:23), who was "before all things and by him all things consist" (Colossians 1:17). To Him who "made himself of no reputation" bearing the humiliation of Calvary for wicked, sinful men who "knowing the judgment of God that they which commit such things are worthy of death not only do the same but have pleasure in them that do them" (Romans 1:32). And to Him who gave Himself for us to redeem us that we might be made "the righteousness of God in him" (2 Corinthians 5:21). All praise to the Great God and our Saviour Jesus Christ.

Deity of Christ Defined

The deity of Christ claims that Jesus of Nazareth and the personal God—the infinite, unchangeable, eternal Creator and Ruler of the Universe—are one and the same and that Jesus the Christ "was God" (John 1:1). "For in him dwelleth all the fulness of the Godhead bodily" (Colossians 2:9). As the International Standard Bible Encyclopedia states: "'Godhead' is the Saxon equivalent of the Latin 'Divinity', or, as it is now becoming more usual to say, 'deity.'"

Gresham Machen defines the deity of Christ as follows: "Now the Christian meaning of the term 'deity of Christ' is fairly clear. The Christian believes that there is a personal God, Creator and Ruler of the universe, a God who is infinite, eternal and unchangeable." Machen continues,

> "So when the Christian says that Jesus Christ is God, or when he says that he believes in the deity of Christ, he means that that same person who is known to history as Jesus of Nazareth existed, before He became man, from all eternity as infinite, eternal and unchangeable God, the second person of the holy Trinity." (Machen, 2017)

Of Christ, in his seminal book on systematic theology, Charles Hodge states:

> "God is not more, and cannot promise more, or do more than Christ is said to be, to promise, and to do. He has, therefore, been the Christian's God from the beginning, in all ages and in all places." (Hodge, 1940, p. 382)

Overall therefore, when we speak of the deity of Christ we are stating that Christ is God, no less or more than the Holy Spirit or the Father, and that in Him dwell all of the constitutional characteristics of the Almighty God, Jehovah. Jesus Christ is God, while at the same time fully man, but without any diminishing of His deity.

Discussion Questions:

1. What is one of the most fundamental truths of our faith?

2. What do we as Christians believe about the Bible?

3. Why is it important to know that Jesus Christ is God?

4. What does the "deity of Christ" mean?

5. Is Christ fully God and fully man? Does being fully man make Him less God?

6. True or false: Jesus Christ our Lord was not only the Son of God but He was also God the Son. Explain.

7. Is Jesus Christ less holy, less omnipotent, less omniscient, less omnipresent, or less eternal than God the Father or God the Holy Ghost?

I. Straightforward Claims of Deity

Within the body of Scripture, the Lord God placed a number of outright, uncontestable claims of the deity of Jesus Christ. The only way one could dispute these claims would be to rewrite the Bible itself, reject it as untrue, or to deny the clear meaning of the Greek and Hebrew text and to refuse to apply standard rules of translation. The accuracy of these claims, however rich in themselves, is clarified and amplified when combined with the weight of the other six issue areas presented in this primer as evidence of the deity of Christ.

For example, John 1:1 is the classic presentation in the Bible of the deity of Christ. "In the beginning was the Word and the Word was with God and the Word was God." Some detractors claim (New World Translation) that there should be an indefinite article before the word "God," therefore changing the reading to "a god"—one of many gods, as opposed to the one and only true God. (The application of Greek rules applying to this text has been an area of great controversy, which we will not deal with in this brief primer.)

On the other hand, there are strong logical arguments that this was properly translated as: "the Word was God." For example, "a god" would imply that there are multiple gods, something that all orthodox Jews and Christians, which are monotheist, would adamantly reject. Also, logic would dictate, that if God were the unique and only Creator of things, how could it be said of a created being that all things were made by Him? "And without Him was not anything made that was made" (John 1:3). In combination with the weight of other evidence, "the Word was God" would appear to be the most logical and consistent interpretation. In John 20:28, the deity of Christ, revealed to us in chapter 1, is re-affirmed by Thomas' assertion, "my Lord and my God." As further affirmation, Jesus not only does not correct Thomas but also says, "Thomas, because thou hast seen me, thou hast believed."

Another text confirming the deity of Christ is found in Acts 20:28, which states: "Take heed therefore unto yourselves, and to all the flock, over the which the Holy Ghost hath made you overseers, to feed the church of God, which he hath purchased with his own blood." As John Gill states, "The purchaser is God, Christ who is God over all" (Gill, 1989). Matthew Henry states: "This proves that Christ is God, for he is called so here, where yet he is said to purchase the church with his own blood" (Henry 1991).

Hebrews 1:8 says, "But unto the Son he saith, Thy throne, O God, is forever and ever: a sceptre of righteousness is the sceptre of thy kingdom." First John 5:20 states:

> "And we know that the Son of God is come, and hath given us an understanding, that we may know him that is true, and we are in him that is true, even in his Son Jesus Christ. This is the true God, and eternal life."

He, Jesus, is the true God and eternal life. As Jesus Himself states in John 10:27-28, "My sheep hear my voice, and I know them, and they follow me: And I give unto them eternal life." Jesus then is the "true God" and "eternal life." In Acts 7:59, the Bible says: "And they stoned Stephen, calling upon God and saying, Lord Jesus, receive my spirit." Stephen called upon

God, the Lord Jesus Christ, and unequivocally identified Jesus as God.

In Isaiah 7:14, the Word of God states: "Therefore the Lord himself shall give you a sign; Behold, a virgin shall conceive, and bear a son, and shall call his name Immanuel." The translation of the Hebrew here is rendered "God with us" or "with us is God." In Matthew 1:23, all doubt as to whom this applies is removed when the Scripture reveals that the prophecy of Isaiah was "fulfilled" in the birth of the Messiah, Jesus. In Isaiah 9:6 He is referred to as "the Mighty God;" in Titus 2:13, "the great God;" and in Acts 10:36, Galatians 4:1, and Romans 10:12 as God over all/Lord of all.

Finally, 2 Peter 1:1 gives clear testimony that Christ is God. This Scripture states: "of God and our Saviour Jesus Christ." In consideration that Isaiah 43:11 states, "I, even I, am the LORD; and beside me there is no saviour," it is clear that "God" refers to the Saviour, Jesus Christ, since there can be no Saviour beside God. The C. Granville Sharp rule of Greek grammar gives further weight to this claim. This rule states that when there are two nouns—neither of which are proper names—which describe a person and are connected by the word "and" (kai), and the first noun (but not the second) has the article "the," then both of the nouns definitely refer to the same person. So, both words, "God" and "Saviour" apply to Jesus Christ. From a Greek grammatical perspective, there is no disputing this interpretation.

Discussion Questions:

1. Which Scripture is considered the classic statement of the deity of Christ? Can you recite it from memory? Can you give arguments to support it?

2. What does Thomas say in John 20:28 that supports the deity of Christ? Can you describe the context? What did Jesus say in response?

3. What do Gill and Henry say about Acts 20:28?

4. Can you tell me the psalm that Hebrews 1:8 was quoting? Does Hebrews 1:8 declare Jesus is God? Does Hebrews 1:2-7 support this view? Explain.

5. Is what is said in Titus 2:13 supportive of the claim of Isaiah 43:11? Explain.

6. How did what Stephen says in Acts 7:59 support the deity of Christ?

7. Use Isaiah 7:14 and Matthew 1:23 to support the deity of Christ.

II. Biblical Prophecy

One of the strongest proofs of the reliability, accuracy and truthfulness of the Bible comes from the record of fulfilled prophecy. Fulfilled prophecy marks the Bible as the divine Word of God. Because of this, we will go into detail about Messianic prophecy in this chapter.

The Bible is full of prophecies that have been fulfilled with incredible pin-point accuracy. Skeptics—those who question the Bible—claim that it was all a coincidence, and that events happened randomly and when Bible prophecy is accurate it is only by chance. Well, we need to examine this claim. Christianity is a reasonable faith that stands up to scrutiny and examination and has, through the years, withstood vicious attacks with great nobility and power. We don't have to hide. We need to be ready always to give an answer. And we can be encouraged that the truth of the Bible is inescapable, indisputable. Unless a person rejects the facts, or lies about them, there is no denying that biblical prophecy has been fulfilled with incredible precision.

The Encyclopedia of Biblical Prophecy claims that there are 1817 biblical prophecies (Payne, 1980). Of these, 1239 are in the Old Testament and the balance of 578 is found in the New Testament. In addition, there are 191 Messianic prophecies within the Hebrew Scriptures of the Old Testament, given to us prior to the writing of the New Testament. Alfred Edersheim identified 456 Old Testament verses about the Messiah or about His times. One might argue that conservatively, in His earthly ministry, Jesus Christ fulfilled at least 300 prophecies. Messianic prophecy is one of the strongest defenses of the deity of Christ, because it demonstrates that the entire plan for the "God-man" Jesus was of divine origin. And His deity was spoken of, heralded, and expected, in some cases, over a thousand years prior to His incarnation.

Since the goal of this book is to present the case for the deity of Christ, God in flesh, it will focus on fulfilled Messianic prophecy. Now the Bible tells us in Deuteronomy 18:22, "when a prophet speaketh in the name of the Lord, if the thing follow not, nor come to pass, that is the thing which the LORD hath not spoken." So the Bible sets up its own standard for the credibility of prophecy. If it does not come to pass, or does not happen, it is not true and not from the LORD. This author maintains that if one researches the claims of biblical prophecy with an open mind and a serious desire for truth, one would find convincing evidence for the claim that these prophecies must have a divine origin.

The best way to present this in a clear fashion is to present the prophecy from the Old Testament Hebrew Scriptures along with the evidence of fulfillment of that prophecy in the life or work of Jesus, the Messiah from the New Testament. In many cases, the writers of the Gospels unambiguously refer to the Old Testament Scripture to explain something about Jesus, saying, "thus it is written by the prophet" or, "that it might be fulfilled which was spoken of the Lord by the prophet," or something to that effect. We will look at a number of these prophecies in detail and then list others for you to research on your own time.

1. "Therefore the Lord himself shall give you a sign; Behold, a virgin shall conceive, and bear a son, and shall call his name Immanuel." (Isaiah 7:14)

It is interesting to note that this Scripture in Isaiah was written about 700 years before the birth of Christ. It prophesies of a young maiden who would conceive a child in a divine way, without an earthly father. And the Scripture says that His name shall be called "Immanuel." The term "Immanuel," "God with us," clearly points to the Messiah of Jewish prophecy.

FULLFILLMENT (Matthew 1:23, Luke 1:27-34)

Please refer to the "Divine Birth" section of this book for a clear exposition of Jesus' virgin birth. He was born as no other man, without an earthly father. He did not inherit our sinful nature and was the sinless Son of God. In Matthew 1:22-23 the Bible says, "that it might be fulfilled which was spoken of the Lord by the prophet, saying…." Matthew continues quoting Isaiah 7:14, clearly identifying Jesus as the fulfillment of that Scripture. The Scripture in Matthew goes on to define "Immanuel" as "God with us." There can be no question that this Scripture establishes the deity of Christ, as a fulfillment of Old Testament prophecy. Jesus was The Word made flesh who dwelt among us—God incarnate.

2. "But thou, Bethlehem Ephratah, though thou be little among the thousands of Judah, yet out of thee shall he come forth unto me that is to be ruler in Israel; whose goings forth have been from of old, from everlasting." (Micah 5:2)

Micah 5:2 predicts that out of Bethlehem will be born a ruler, whose origin is from the days of eternity. As one commentator

15

explains the Greek meaning of "from old, from everlasting" could be defined as: "Not from the world but from the beginning, not in the days of time, but from the days of eternity."

FULLFILLMENT (Matthew 2:1, Luke 2:1-6, John 7:42)

In Matthew 2:1 the Scripture says, "Now when Jesus was born in Bethlehem of Judaea." Luke 2:1-6 relates the story of His birth in a manger in Bethlehem as Joseph and Mary travelled to this city due to a census being taken at that time. Joseph was of the house of David and Bethlehem was the City of David. And John 7:42 confirms the Jewish prophecy that the Messiah would be "of the seed of David, and out of the town of Bethlehem, where David was." And Jesus was from everlasting to everlasting, the eternal Son of God. As it says in John 1:1, "In the beginning was the Word and the Word was with God and the Word was God. The same was in the beginning with God."

3. "For dogs have compassed me: the assembly of the wicked have inclosed me: they pierced my hands and my feet." (Psalm 22:16; also see Zechariah 12:10)

Psalm 22 prophesies many things about the Messiah. The time of writing was likely around 1,000 years before the birth of Christ. But here it predicts His death by crucifixion. And this was at a time when the Jewish mode of execution was by stoning. Crucifixion may have originated with the Assyrians and Babylonians but there is no evidence that it was ever used by Jews. It was many years later that the Romans perfected this specific, horrific form of torture and execution by impalement called crucifixion. The Scripture says His hands and feet would be pierced. Zechariah 12:10 says, "they shall look upon me whom they have pierced, and they shall mourn for him, as one mourneth for his only son." The crucifixion of Jesus is not in dispute and is one of the best documented killings in history. God sent His only begotten Son to die for us on a cross, "that whosoever believeth in Him shall not perish but have everlasting life" (John 3:16).

FULLFILLMENT (Matthew 27:31, Mark 15:20, John 19:15-16)

Most scholars, Christian and secular, would agree that the death of Jesus Christ by crucifixion is one of the most highly supported facts of ancient history. It is indisputable. Jesus was crucified. In crucifixion, metal nails were driven through the hands and feet of the victim. The scriptural account clearly supports this fact. Matthew 27:31 and Mark 15:20 both say that they led Jesus away to crucify Him. And John 19:15-16 states, "Then Pilate gave Jesus to them to be crucified."

4. "He was oppressed, and he was afflicted, yet he opened not his mouth: he is brought as a lamb to the slaughter, and as a sheep before her shearers is dumb, so he openeth not his mouth." (Isaiah 53:7)

This Scripture is from Isaiah and the entire chapter is known as the great prophecy of the suffering servant and is accepted by both messianic Jews and Christians as a prophecy of the Messiah. It predicts that when the Messiah is afflicted, or caused pain or suffering, He would be silent, as a lamb being slaughtered.

FULLFILLMENT (Matthew 27:12-14, Mark 15:4-5, 1 Peter 2:22-23)

Matthew 27:12-14 tells us that when the Messiah Jesus was questioned by the chief priests and elders, "He answered nothing." "Then said Pilate unto him, hearest thou not how many things they witness against thee? And He answered them never a word." This is also supported by Mark 15:4-5. And in 1 Peter 2:22-23 we read of Jesus: "Who did no sin, neither was guile found in his mouth: Who, when he was reviled, reviled not again; when he suffered, he threatened not."

5. "Rejoice greatly, O daughter of Zion; shout, O daughter of Jerusalem: behold, thy King cometh unto thee: he is just, and having salvation; lowly, and riding upon an ass, and upon a colt the foal of an ass." (Zechariah 9:9)

The book of Zechariah was written around 530 BC. The main purpose of the book was to motivate and encourage the Jews who had returned from Babylon to continue to rebuild the Temple. They were facing constant opposition to this task. The final part of the book foretells the struggles God's people would face in the world. But it then encourages them with the hope of the coming Messiah who would destroy those forces that stand against the Kingdom of God. In this Scripture we see pictured the rejoicing of God's people in the coming of the lowly and humble Messiah, who would bring salvation, riding into Jerusalem on a donkey.

FULFILLMENT (Matthew 21:4-11, Luke 19:35-40, John 12:12-15)

The triumphal journey of our Saviour Jesus Christ, known as Palm Sunday, is recounted in churches each year across the world. Scripture clearly outlines this historical event. In

Matthew 21 Jesus tells His disciples, "Go into the village over against you, and straight-way ye shall find an ass tied, and a colt with her: loose them, and bring them unto me." The Scripture then declares that this event was a fulfillment of Zechariah 9:9 as verse 4 says: "All this was done, that it might be fulfilled which was spoken by the prophet" and then references Zechariah 9:9. Then Luke and John recount the same story with Jesus mounting the donkey and the multitude spreading their "clothes in the way" along with palm branches. In Matthew, similar to Luke's account, the multitude cried out, "Hosanna to the Son of David: Blessed is he that cometh in the name of the Lord; Hosanna in the highest."

6. "Yea, mine own familiar friend, in whom I trusted, which did eat of my bread, hath lifted up his heel against me." (Psalm 41:9)

David writes this psalm, under the inspiration of God, about his own distresses and betrayals. But it also has a future application, as prophecies do, to the coming Messiah. This Messianic psalm warns that the Messiah Jesus would be betrayed by a close friend, someone He trusted and with whom He would share bread.

FULFILLMENT (Matthew 26:47-50; Luke 22:21-22, 47-48; John 13:18, 21, 26)

So how can we know for certain that this Scripture is applied by God to the Messiah Jesus? In John 13:18, Jesus says, "but now that the Scripture may be fulfilled, He that eateth bread with me hath lifted up his heel against me." It was Judas Iscariot that betrayed Him, as he was the one that came to the garden with "a great multitude with swords and staves, from the chief priests and elders." Judas, the betrayer, gave them a sign. The night was dark and, so no mistake could be made, he said, "whomsoever I shall kiss the same is he." Jesus considered Judas as a disciple and as a friend. Jesus said unto him, "Friend, wherefore are thou come?"

7. "They part my garments among them, and cast lots upon my vesture." (Psalm 22:18)

Messianic Psalm 22:18 predicts that the Saviour's clothes, His garments, would be divided and gambled for. Obviously referring to the actions of the coming Messiah's enemies the Scripture says they will "part" His clothing and "cast lots" for them.

FULFILLMENT (Matthew 27:35, Mark 15:24, John 19:23-24)

Matthew 27:35 clearly states: "And they crucified him, and parted his garments, casting lots." And to make certain there is no mistake that this was fulfilled prophecy, the Scripture continues: "that it might be fulfilled which was spoken by the prophet," referring to David's Psalm 22. The Gospel of Mark 15:24 also says they "parted his garments casting lots upon them." And in John, we find one final unambiguous support for fulfilled prophecy. In John 19:23-24 we find the reason for not parting the garment, that it had no seam and that they gambled for it instead. But in verse 24 John says, "that the Scripture might be fulfilled" and then quotes Psalm 22 to show that this was the Messianic prophecy and it was fulfilled in Messiah Jesus.

8. "He keepeth all his bones: not one of them is broken." (Psalm 34:20)

Exodus chapter 12 recounts the story of how God took the life of all the first-born Egypt as a final plague against the disobedience of Pharaoh and the sin of Egypt. Israel was protected from this judgment. They were commanded by God to kill an unblemished male lamb of the first year and place its blood on the two sides and upper door posts of their houses. And when the death angel came, it passed over all those people who were hiding in their houses, houses which had blood on them in the prescribed way. The blood protected them but not the Egyptians. As a result, Pharaoh let them leave Egypt. If we refer back to the ninth chapter of the book of Numbers and the establishment of the Passover feast, the application to the Saviour becomes very clear. Numbers 9:12 recounts how in observance of the Passover, the Jews were to kill and eat the Passover lamb, but "they shall leave none of it unto the morning, nor break any bone of it."

FULFILLMENT (John 19:31-36, 1 Corinthians 5:7)

As the Scripture says in 1 Corinthians 5:7, "For even Christ our Passover lamb is sacrificed for us." Christ, the Lamb of God, our Passover Lamb, whose blood was shed for the sins of the world, with the cross of Calvary as His altar, not one of His bones were broken. John 19:31-36 relates how after a crucifixion, it was the practice to break the legs of victims of crucifixion to insure they had died. The soldiers broke the legs of the two criminals crucified with Jesus. "But when they came to Jesus, and saw that he was dead already, they brake not his legs."

9. "For thou wilt not leave my soul in hell; neither wilt thou suffer thine Holy One to see corruption." (Psalm 16:10)

The prophet/king David was born around 1000 years before Christ. In Psalm 16:10 he prophesied that the Messiah's body would be resurrected out of the grave and not see the decay of His body after death, a process which the bodies of mortal men all experience.

FULLFILLMENT (Acts 2:27-31, Matthew 28:5-7, Mark 16:6-7, 1 Corinthians 15:17)

Acts 2:27 firmly establishes that this Scripture is applied, by the Word of God, to Jesus Christ. In verse 31, Peter's sermon at Pentecost quotes Psalm 16:10 in support of the deity of Christ. Peter preached that God did "raise up Christ to sit on his throne…He seeing this before spake of the resurrection of Christ" and again quotes Psalm 16:10 as support. After the crucifixion, the body of Christ was removed from the cross and put into a tomb hewn in the rock. The Scriptures in Matthew 28:6 and Mark 16:6 describe the scene when the women visited the tomb and met an angel who told them, "He is not here: for he is risen." That this resurrection was true was attested to not only by the disciples and women who saw the risen Jesus on a number of occasions, but by over 500 others who also saw the resurrected Saviour over a 40-day period. This was clearly a fulfillment of prophecy.

10. "They gave me also gall for my meat; and in my thirst they gave me vinegar to drink." (Psalm 69:21)

This is another psalm written by the prophet/king David, born about 1000 years before Christ. As with prophecy, there is normally a present application and a future application. In this case David speaks to his present situation and God speaks through him about the coming Messiah. In verse 20 the psalmist says "Reproach hath broken my hear: and I am full of heaviness: And I looked for some to take pity, but there was none; and for comforters, but I found none." In this messianic psalm, God then speaks through David and reveals that Jesus will be given gall and vinegar to drink by His persecutors.

FULLFILLMENT (Matthew 27:34, John 19:28-30)

In Matthew 27:34 we have the scene of Jesus, taken to Golgotha, the Place of the Skull, to be crucified. There the soldiers "gave him vinegar to drink mingled with gall." And in John 19:28, Jesus is in His last moments of life on earth. Here He exclaims, "I thirst." And the Scripture says, "and they filled a spunge with vinegar and put it upon hyssop, and put it to his mouth."

Conclusion to Biblical Prophecy

Although a controversial figure, the work of Dr. Peter Stoner may give us an unusual yet useful perspective on prophecy and probability.   Dr. Peter Stoner was Chairman of the Departments of Mathematics and Astronomy at Pasadena City College until 1953; Chairman of the science division, Westmont College, 1953–57; and Professor Emeritus of Science, Westmont College. He looked specifically at eight of the Messianic prophecies with the idea of calculating the probability that all eight of these prophecies would come true by chance, by accident. Here are his astounding results.

He estimated that the probability or possibility that even eight of these prophecies could be fulfilled by chance, by accident, is one in 100,000,000,000,000,000 (or one in one hundred quadrillion).   The chance of being struck with lightning in any year is a mere one in 700,000. My friend, fulfilled Messianic prophecy is not by chance, could not have been by chance, and was truly the work of God. The fulfilled prophecies cry out with the truth! He is the Messiah, the Anointed One, the Saviour of the world! God took on flesh and came to earth and subjected Himself to humiliation and torture, bearing your sins to the cross and paying your sin debt. And He did it for the joy, as it says in Hebrews 12:2, because He loves you and because He knows you need a Saviour. That is God's grace.

Here we have not even covered prophecies from the New Testament, which were fulfilled with astounding accuracy. For example, in Mark 10:33-34 Jesus prophesies his own resurrection saying, "and they shall mock him and scourge him, and shall spit upon him, and shall kill him: and the third day he shall rise again." In Luke 21:20-24, Matthew 24:1-3, and Mark 13:3-4, Jesus predicts the sacking of Rome by the Romans which would not occur until decades after His death in 70 AD, describing it with surprising accuracy. He says in Mark 13:1: "Seest thou these great buildings? There shall not be left on stone upon another, that shall not be thrown down." The ancient historian Josephus actually witnessed the attack in 70 AD. He reported that Caesar gave orders to demonish the city and the temple. The Romans did, but after they had no more people to slay, in their hateful zeal they even dug up the foundations to make it appear that nothing had ever existed (Josephus, 2013). This is precisely as Jesus predicted.

Many other fulfilled prophecies attest to the divine person of Jesus Christ our Messiah. But we do not have time to go through each. Suffice it to say that the weight of evidence of fulfilled prophecy is so astounding, so overwhelming, that any unbiased unbeliever would be led to re-examine their beliefs and consider Christ. And any believer would be led to stand up and cheer, "Hosanna in the Highest!" Please remember that, although there are scores of Messianic prophecies are which are clear and indisputable, there are some which may be more tangential and unclear. But don't let some which are initially harder to understand detract from massive body of clear and fulfilled prophecy evident in the Word of God. For a list of a number of other prophecies relating to the Messiah Jesus for the reader to further their research, please refer to the Appendix Table 1.

Discussion Questions:

1. According to *Encyclopedia of Biblical Prophecy* how many biblical prophecies have been identified in the Bible? How many prophecies of the coming Messiah, Jesus Christ, are there in the Old Testament?

2. Which Gospel was written to the Jews to prove that Christ was the awaited Messiah? Which Gospel was written to the Romans? Which was written to the Greeks? And which of the four Gospels was considered the Gospel of the deity of Christ?

3. What does Isaiah 53 predict about the coming Christ? Was it true about Christ?

4. List six Old Testament Scriptures that are prophecies of the coming Christ and tell what each predicts about Jesus and how they were fulfilled.

5. Discuss Psalm 22 and three things that it predicts about the coming Messiah that were fulfilled in Jesus Christ.

6. Discuss Isaiah 9:6 in terms of the deity of Christ. Can you recite it from memory?

7. Why could it be said that it takes a great deal of faith to reject biblical prophecy?

III. His Divine Names and Titles

The most powerful argument for the deity of Christ is one that incensed the Jewish leaders. Christ identified Himself with the Old Testament titles and names for God and permitted others to call Him by them (McDowell & Larson, 1983). As R. A. Torrey states:

> "The first line of proof of the absolute deity of our Lord Jesus is that many names and titles clearly implying deity are used of Jesus Christ in the Bible, some of them over and over again, the total number of passages reaching far into the hundreds." (Torrey, 1918, p. 76)

Even the name "Jesus" itself, given by the Angel of the Lord to the babe born of the Virgin Mary, announces the God-man, Jesus Christ our Saviour. It is the Greek form of Jeshua or Joshua, the meaning of which is "Jehovah-Saviour" or "the Lord Saves."

Although not intended to be exhaustive, what follows is a list of names chosen to illustrate the fact that Jesus unreservedly used and was called by names reserved for Jehovah God.

I AM

Jesus himself claimed the name of God most highly revered by the Jews, considered so sacred that the Jews wouldn't even utter it or write it out completely. They would write "YHWH" (Yahweh or Jehovah). In Exodus 3:13 Moses is complaining to God about the task God has given him and unconfident of facing the Jews and telling them that the God of their Fathers "hath sent me unto you." He asks God how he should answer them if they ask "What is His name?" God tells him to say, "I AM THAT I AM" (verse 14). This "I AM" has been translated from the Hebrew word *Hayah*, meaning to become, to exist, the existent one. However Hebrew scholars also say it can mean "the God who is the God," *Yah*, meaning God. In the Septuagint Greek translation of the Hebrew Old Testament, the Jewish translators translated the "I AM" in Exodus 3:14 into the Greek as *ego eimi*.

Clearly it was their opinion that this Greek word best captured the meaning of this title God took to Himself. One meaning which can be applied to *ego eimi* is the pre-existent, unchanging eternal being (Barnes, 1983). The Received Text (Textus Receptus) translates the instance in the Greek New Testament, where Jesus referred to himself as "I AM" in John 8:57-58 also as *ego eimi*. So both the Greek translation of the Hebrew Old Testament by Jewish scholars as well as the Greek translation of this passage in the New Testament agree. It is clear Jesus was claiming the name which God had given to Himself, as the "I AM," the pre-existent, eternal, unchanging one, the one true God. Jews, understanding this, reacted by desiring to stone Him for the sacrilege of referring to Himself as Jehovah. Stoning was the Old Testament punishment for blasphemy (Leviticus 24:16). In other words, Christ unambiguously referred to Himself as the Jehovah God.

The Lord

This title, "Lord," is used for Jesus several hundred times in the New Testament. Although used nine times in the New Testament to refer to men, it was never used in this way when referring to Jesus (Torrey, 1918, p. 56). In the Old Testament, it is first used in Genesis 2:4, and used hundreds of times to refer to Jehovah God. In Ezekiel the compound term "the Lord God" is used 16 times to refer to Jehovah, connecting both terms for God, Jehovah and Elohim. The term "Lord" (*kurios*) is used as a divine name also when applied to Jesus. For example, in Philippians 2:11, Jehovah God commands that "every tongue should confess, that Jesus Christ is Lord, to the glory of the Father." In Acts 10:36, the Word of God states of Jesus Christ that "he is Lord of all." First Corinthians 2:8, when referring to those who took part in the death of Christ, states: "for had they known it, they would not have crucified the Lord of Glory."

First and the Last

"The First and the Last" is another powerful example of names/titles used for Christ, proclaiming Christ's deity. In Revelation 1:13 the Scripture says: "And in the midst of the seven candlesticks one like unto the Son of man, clothed with a garment down to the foot, and girt about the paps with a golden girdle." The passage in Revelation 1:17-18 continues:

> "And when I saw him, I fell at his feet as dead. And he laid his right hand upon me, saying unto me, Fear not; I am the first and the last: I am he that liveth, and was dead; and, behold , I am alive for evermore, Amen; and have the keys of hell and of death."

Clearly, "Son of man" and "he that liveth, and was dead; and, behold, I am alive for evermore" refer to the Son of God. Jesus is the focus of the book of Revelation, and it is Christ our Lord who died but "rose again the third day" (1 Corinthians 15:4). Therefore, the passage above clearly identifies Jesus as the "first and the last." However, in Isaiah 44:6 we read: "Thus saith the LORD the King of Israel, and his redeemer the LORD of hosts; I am the first, and I am the last; and beside me there is no God." The word "LORD" used here in the Hebrew is the word for "Jehovah." There is no other God beside Jehovah and He is the first and the last. Therefore, since the Scriptures declare Christ Jesus as the First and the Last, a title reserved exclusively for Jehovah God, the Scriptures articulate unambiguously that Christ is Jehovah God.

Lord of Lords

In Revelation 17:14 the Lamb, referring to Christ Jesus, is called "the Lord of lords and King of kings." Once again Jesus is referred to with the same name in 1 Timothy 6:15. In Deuteronomy 10:17, Jehovah is referred to as "God of gods, and Lord of lords." This also argues for Christ's divinity. As McDowell and Larson argue, if the passage in 1 Timothy refers to God, then God and Christ share the same titles; "Lord of lords," which Jesus, the Lamb, is clearly named in Revelation 17:14. If it is about Christ, which it appears clear it is, then He shares other titles with God including "Who only hath immortality" and "only Potentate" (Mcdowell & Larson, 1983). Either way, these passages confirm the deity of Christ.

Saviour and Redeemer

In Titus 2:14, Galatians 4:5, Ephesians 1:7, and Hebrews 9:12, Christ is identified as the one by whose blood we are redeemed, who "gave himself for us that he might redeem us," the Saviour and Redeemer. In the Old Testament, Jehovah is the one who will "redeem Israel from all his iniquities." In Psalm 78:35 He is referred to as "God their redeemer." In Isaiah 41:14 and 43:14, as well as in Isaiah 47:4 and 48:17, God is referred to as "thy redeemer, the Holy One of Israel." Jesus Christ our Lord shares this title with Jehovah God.

The Word of God also clearly applies the name "Saviour" to Jesus Christ our Lord, a name reserved to be given exclusively to God in the Old Testament. In Isaiah 43:11; 45:21 and Hosea 13:4, Jehovah God is our Saviour and the only Saviour. As it states in Isaiah 43:11: "I, even I, am the LORD; and beside me there is no Saviour." In Isaiah 49:26 the Word of God states: "I the Lord am thy Saviour and the Redeemer, the mighty one of Jacob" (see also Isaiah 60:16). In Luke 19:10 Jesus declares, "For the Son of man is come to seek and to save that which was lost." Luke 2:11 asserts it even more clearly: "For unto you is born this David in the city of David a Saviour, which is Christ the Lord."

Particularly interesting are the three couplets revealed in the book of Titus. In the first couplet in Titus 1:3 the Bible states, "God our Savior;" however, in the following verse it states, "the Lord Jesus Christ our Savior." A second couplet is found in chapter two where in verse ten the Bible declares, "God our Savior in all things" where three verses later it declares, "the great God and our Savior Jesus Christ." The final couplet is found in the third chapter. In verse four we find "the love of God our Savior" but in verse six we once again find "Jesus Christ our Savior." Applying the rule of biblical interpretation, this triple display of identical couplets in Titus with first God as Saviour and then Jesus as Saviour, gives crystal clear evidence that God and Jesus are one and the same. In each of the three chapters in Titus, the name which is only to be applied to God is applied to God and alternately to Jesus. What a powerful testimony to the deity of Jesus Christ our Lord.

Finally, Acts 4:12 boldly declares, related to the Lord Jesus, that there is no salvation in any other person, "for there is none other name under heaven given among men, whereby we must be saved." Therefore since many passages in the Old Testament, such as Isaiah 43:11, declare that there is no Saviour besides God, then it follows that if Jesus is also declared Saviour in the Word of God, He must also be God.

Light

Another title used for both God and Jesus Christ is "light." In John 1:4 Jesus is "the light of men." In John 3:19 He is referred to as "light" which has "come into the world." In John 9:5 Jesus Christ self-professes, "I am the light of the world." However, Psalm 27:1 states: "The Lord is my light and my salvation." This shows Jesus is referred to as both light and salvation. Isaiah 60:20 says: "for the LORD shall be thine everlasting light." Jesus shares the name of light with Jehovah.

The Truth

In John 14:6 Jesus states that He is "the way, the truth and the life." He refers to Himself emphatically as the truth. In John 1:17 the Bible states: "For the law was given by Moses, but grace and truth came by Jesus Christ." In Revelation 19:11 Christ is referred to as the one on a white horse "called Faithful and True." Verse 13 makes it clear that this is referring to Jesus, "The Word of God." Note that "Faithful and True" is capitalized and is therefore a title, a name given to Jesus. In Psalm 31:5, Jehovah is referred to as "O Lord God of truth." Deuteronomy 32:4 calls God "a God of truth." In Psalm 25:5, David asks God to "lead me in thy truth." This term, "thy truth" referring to God's truth, is used in the Book of Psalms fourteen times.

It is clear that God is truth as Jesus is truth, because Jesus is God.

Judge of All

Hebrews 12:23 refers to God as "Judge of all." The word "Judge" is capitalized, being a title given to Jehovah. In Psalm 50:4-6, God judges His people. In Psalm 96:13, Jehovah "shall judge the world with righteousness and the people with his truth." Christ shares that name with God, pointing clearly to His divinity. In John 5:22, the Bible says that God "hath committed all judgment unto the Son." In Romans 14:10 and 2 Corinthians 5:10 the Scriptures refer to the "judgment seat of Christ." In Matthew 25:31-46, it is Jesus who judges, sitting on the throne of His glory. Second Timothy 4:1 states: "I charge thee therefore before God, and the Lord Jesus Christ, who shall judge the quick and the dead at his appearing and his kingdom." God shall judge the world and to Jesus ALL judgment is committed. Jesus shares the title and prerogatives as "judge of all" with God.

Shepherd

Christ is our Shepherd, a term repeatedly used for the Lord Jehovah in the Old and New Testaments. In Psalm 23:1 it is written, "The Lord is my shepherd; I shall not want." In Psalm 80:1 the Lord Jehovah is referred to as "O Shepherd of Israel." In Psalm 100:3 Israel is seen as "his people, and the sheep of his pasture." Referring to Christ's return, 1 Peter 5:4 talks of "and when the chief Shepherd shall appear." In John 10:11, 14 Jesus refers to Himself as "the good shepherd." Jesus, in John 10:27, calls them "my sheep" who "hear my voice." Jesus is the Good Shepherd, the Lord who is our Shepherd, who gives eternal life to His sheep.

Creator

Finally, Jesus Christ shares the title "Creator" with the Lord Jehovah, a compelling indication of His deity. "In the beginning God created the heaven and the earth" (Genesis 1:1). Psalm 102:25 relates how Jehovah God laid the foundations of the earth and "the heavens are the work of thy hands." In the New Testament, these same words are repeated in Hebrews 1:10. However, here it refers to Jesus, the Son of God. This was a continuation of the speech, the conversation about Jesus begun in Hebrews 1:8 (Gill, 1989). In John 1:1-3 the Bible tells us:

> "In the beginning was the Word, and the Word was with God, and the Word was God. The same was in the beginning with God. All things were made by him; and without him was not anything made that was made."

And in Colossians 1:15-16 the Bible relates, referring to Jesus:

> "Who is the image of the invisible God, the firstborn of every creature: For by him were all things created, that are in heaven, and that are in earth, visible and invisible, whether they be thrones, or dominions, or principalities, or powers: all things were created by him, and for him."

Therefore, Jesus Christ our Lord is given the name of Creator God. It was by His hands as God, that the God/Man was Creator of the universe and was before all, uncreated and eternal existent.

Discussion Questions:

1. What is considered one of the most powerful arguments for the deity of Christ, and why did it anger the Jews?

2. Compare Exodus 3:14 with John 8:58. How does this support the deity of Christ?

3. In Isaiah 44:6, who does God say is the first and the last? Who does Revelation 1:17-18 say is the first and the last? How does this support the deity of Christ?

4. In Isaiah 43:11 and Hosea 13:4, who does God say is the only Saviour? Who does Luke 2:11, 2 Timothy 1:10, 2 Peter 1:11 say is the Saviour? How does this support the deity of Christ?

5. Explain why the three couplets in Titus 1, 2, and 3 are so   interesting. How do they support the deity of Christ?

6. Compare Hebrews 12:23 and Psalm 96:13 with 2 Timothy 4:1 and Romans 14:10. According to Hebrews and Psalms, who is the Judge of all the earth? But according to Timothy and Romans who is/will be judge? How does this support the deity of Christ?

7. Compare Genesis 1:1 with John 1:3 and Colossians 1:16. Who is Creator in Genesis? Who is Creator in John and Colossians? How does this support the deity of Christ?

IV. What Jesus Says about Himself

This section reveals what Jesus claimed about Himself. Since this book is based on the assumption that the Bible is the infallible truth of the Word of God, we can assume the Bible is reliable. And since the Bible is the revelation of God regarding His Son Jesus Christ, we can claim that whatever Jesus clearly articulates takes on a special significance.

As Machen points out, another clear indication of Jesus' claim to deity is that in the gospel Jesus preached, He Himself was the main character, the way and truth and life, the resurrection, the I AM. The gospel of Jesus was also a gospel about Jesus; the gospel that He preached was also a gospel that offered Him as Saviour (Machen, 2017).

Believe Also in Me

Jesus did not say merely: "Have faith in God like the faith that I have in God," but He said: "Have faith in me" (Machen, 2017). In John 14:1 Jesus says, "ye believe in God, believe also in me," inextricably linking faith in Jehovah God and faith in Him. In John 11:26 Christ turns all eyes to Him and whoever "believeth in me shall never die." Belief in Christ is the source of eternal life and healing (John 11:26, Luke 8:48). Belief in Christ is the source of fulfillment (John 6:35). The story of the Bible is centered on Christ. The foundation of the gospel and of the Bible is Christ. It is faith in Christ and Christ alone that separates the condemned sinner from the saved saint.

They Are My Sheep

About His saved saints, in John 10:27 Jesus says, "My sheep hear my voice and I know them, and they follow me: And I give unto them eternal life." In both John 10:3 and 4, Jesus says they are "his own sheep." But Psalm 95:7 proclaims God's elect as "the people of His pasture, and the sheep of His hand," and Psalm 100:3 "His people and the sheep of His pasture." In Ezekiel 34:31 Jehovah God asserts "And Ye my flock, the flock of my pasture." Jesus boldly declares that, as the second person of the Trinity, God the Son, these sheep are His, given to Him by the Father (John 10:29).

I Am the Way the Truth and the Life

Another of Christ's claims in the Word of God is that He is the Way and the Truth and the Life (John 14:6). He is the "door of the sheep," a door which if anyone enters "he shall be saved" (John 10:7-9). He is the narrow path to heaven (Matthew 7:13-14). He is the truth that sets us free from the law of sin and death (Romans 8:2), and gives eternal life (1 John 5:12). At the same time Psalm 25:4-5 states, speaking of the Lord God: "Show me thy ways, O LORD; teach me thy paths. Lead me in thy truth, and teach me: for thou art the God of my salvation" (see also Psalm 86:11). So God is the Way (path), the Truth and the Life (salvation). Jesus clearly is the source of divine gifts that only Jehovah God can claim to give. Christ Himself claims to be the source of these gifts, the Way, the Truth, and the Life.

Knowing Jesus Is Knowing the Father

Jesus unambiguously asserts His deity in John 8:19, saying, "if ye had known me, ye should have known my Father also." Here, Jesus doesn't say "if ye had known my Father" you would know Him, instead He asserts that if you know JESUS you "should have known the Father also." Knowledge of the *logos*, the Son, leads to knowledge of Jehovah God. He is the Way. And He has exclusive right to knowledge and access to the Father. No man "cometh to the Father but by me" (John 14:6). Therefore, no man can know or have access to the Father but by the Son, and He and the Father are one (John 10:30).

I Am the Bread of Life

In John 6:51 Jesus asserts, "I am the living bread which came down from heaven; if any man eat of this bread he shall live forever." In verse 54 he says, "Whoso eateth my flesh and drinketh my blood, hath eternal life; and I will raise him up at the last day." Jesus doesn't claim that God gives eternal life through Him, but it is by Jesus that they receive eternal life; He will raise them up. Fully man, fully God, the Christ as God does the work of God.

Blessed Are Those Persecuted "for My Sake"

In Matthew 5:11 Jesus states: "Blessed are ye, when men shall revile you, and persecute you, and shall say all manner of evil against you falsely, for my sake." He goes on to say that those who do get persecuted for his name should rejoice in it, for their reward will be great in heaven. Jesus says His followers will be hated "for my name's sake," and those who will endure it will be saved (Matthew 10:22). In Matthew 10:39 Jesus Christ our Lord says that losing one's life "for my sake" results in finding everlasting life. He did not make a distinction between Him and God, but claimed equality with God in claiming that those who suffer for Him, Jesus Christ, would receive a reward in heaven. He claimed He would be the reason for and had the prerogative to award heavenly rewards.

Whosever Shall Be Ashamed of Me

In Luke 14:26 Jesus says, "If any man come to me, and hate not his father, and mother, and wife, and children, and brethren, and sisters, yea, and his own life also, he cannot be my disciple." And this is the same Jesus who in Mark 8:38 claimed:

> "Whosoever therefore shall be ashamed of me and of my words in this adulterous and sinful generation; of him also shall the Son of man be ashamed, when he cometh in the glory of his Father with the holy angels."

As Machen emphatically points out:

> "Who can claim such an exclusive devotion as that—a devotion which shall take precedence of even the holiest of earthly ties, a devotion upon which a man's eternal destiny depends? God can, but can any mere man?" (Machen, 2017, p. 16)

Judge

In John 5:22 Jesus says that the Father "committed all judgment unto the Son." In Romans 2:16, "God shall judge the secrets of men by Jesus Christ according to my gospel." And Isaiah 33:22 states, "For the LORD is our judge, the LORD is our lawgiver, the LORD is our king; he will save us." So Christ claimed He is Judge as God is Judge and that He is Saviour as God is Saviour.

That All Men Should Honour the Son, Even as They Honour the Father

John 5:23 declares: "That all men should honour the Son, even as they honour the Father. He that honoureth not the Son honoureth not the Father which hath sent him." Jesus makes it clear here that He is worthy to receive honor, the honor reserved for the Father. And later in the chapter (verse 39) Jesus maintains that the Scriptures are those that testify of Him, and that to receive the eternal life from the eternal book, men must come to Him.

Epilogue IV: What Jesus Says about Himself

In this chapter, we have provided biblical evidence that supports that Jesus makes the astounding claim that He is God, the *logos*, the Word in John 1 who "was God," the Creator, without whom was not anything made that was made. He Himself claims these things about Himself. In summary:

- Jesus tells us to believe in Jesus, like we do in the Father. If He were not God then He would be contradicting the first two commandments and asking them to practice idolatry.
- Jesus claims that if you believe in Him you will never die.
- Jesus claims that the saints of God are His sheep. They are His sheep and they follow Him and that He, Jesus, gives them eternal life.
- Jesus claims He is the Way (*hodos* in Greek), the Truth, and the Life, and no man can have access to the Father but by Jesus. He is the door to heaven and the only door. And what He says is true

because He is truth. And through Him is life, which only the Creator can give.

- Jesus claims that knowing Him is knowing the Father and that seeing Jesus is seeing the Father, because they are one and the same. In fact, later in John 14:8, Philip asks Jesus, "Lord show us the Father and it sufficeth us." To that question Jesus answers, "Have I been so long time with you, and yet hast thou not known me, Philip? <u>He that hath seen me hath seen the Father</u>" (emphasis added).

- Jesus claims that He is the bread of life. Jesus is the living bread. And if a man eats of that bread "he shall live forever."

- Jesus claims He has the power to resurrect dead people to eternal life.

- Jesus claimed that whoever suffered for Him and His name would receive a reward in heaven. In Matthew 16:24-28, the words of our Saviour tell us that to follow Him we must take up our bitter cross and follow Him, to deny ourselves for Him, and if called upon, to die for Him. He then tells us that He shall come in the glory of the Father and He shall reward men according to their works. And that they shall see Him coming in His, Jesus', Kingdom.

- Jesus claims devotion to Himself above all earthy relations including family and that devotion to Him determines our eternal destiny.

- Jesus claims to be the Judge of the world. This is something that only God, or someone who claims to be God, could claim.

- Jesus claims He is worthy of the honor given to God. He says that men should honor and devote their lives to Him, just as they honor and devote their lives to the Father.

The historical evidence is overwhelming in support what Jesus says about Himself. For example, Jesus calls Himself the Resurrection and the Life (John 11:25) and predicted His own resurrection (Mark 9:31, Matthew 27:63). And 500 people witnessed His resurrection during a period of 40 days. And what is astounding is the lack of any historical evidence; no record that any of those people ever denied seeing the resurrected Christ, even though they had many years during which they could have. And His disciples who supposedly witnessed His resurrection and ascension were later persecuted and tortured. Many of them died the most gruesome painful deaths, in defense of this faith. In fact history tells us that all the apostles were eventually martyred except for the Apostle John, who himself was exiled to the island of Patmos where he died. And Peter was martyred just as Jesus predicted, being crucified—at Peter's request, as history tells us—upside down. It goes against all logic that these Jewish converts, reasonable men, would all gives their lives for a lie, if they did not believe Jesus was who He claimed He was, God's Son and God the Son.

With this in mind, it would be good to examine a little further these claims of deity by Jesus of Himself. First of all we need to examine whether or not the Jesus of the Bible was just a legend and not the same Jesus as the one who lived on the earth about 2,000 years ago. This is highly improbable if not unthinkable for a number of reasons. First of all, we must remember that Jesus grew up as a Jew of Israel, the one nation that was convinced that there was only one God, as the Shema, their most holy prayer states. C. S. Lewis argues that it would be very odd that this invention, this legend of a religious leader should develop among "the one people in the whole earth least likely to make such a mistake" (Lewis, 2015). In fact, the Bible demonstrates that it wasn't easy for His followers to believe He was God. Peter denied Him, Judas betrayed Him, His disciples denied and forsook Him in the garden when the soldiers took Him. Even Thomas did not declare Him to be God until after He saw the risen Christ and then exclaimed "My Lord and my God."

And in His discourse in John chapter 6, Jesus, speaking to many disciples (not just the apostles) says these amazing words: "He that eateth my flesh and drinketh my blood dwelleth in me and I in Him," and "he that eateth of this bread shall live forever." The disciples murmured about it, saying "that is an hard saying; who can hear it." And when He sensed their unbelief, Jesus said, "Doth this offend you...what if you see the Son of Man ascend up where he was before." This is a clear claim of deity. And the Bible tells us because of this "many of his disciples went back, and walked no more with him."

It was certainly peculiar, it was strange, that such a legend would arise among Israel and regarding one of their own people, a Jew. In fact, the honesty of the Bible militates against the idea that the Bible was a fabricated lie. It would have been easy to hide Peter's denial, Judas' betrayal, the weakness of faith of the disciples. But the Bible is honest and truthful, leaving none of this out of the inspired Word of God. And as C. S. Lewis argues, the Gospels are nothing like literary legends. They leave out much of the life of Jesus. They just do not have the artistic or literary style of a legend (Lewis, 2015).

So where does this leave us. If it is not a legend, then who is this Jesus? In his 1936 book *Normal Christian Faith* (Nee, 1997), Watchman Nee sets out for us three options:

- First, if Jesus claims to be God and yet in fact is not, He has to be a madman or a lunatic.
- Second, if He is neither God nor a lunatic, He has to be a liar, deceiving others by His lie.
- Third, if He is neither of these, He must be God.

As Nee states: "There is no need for us to prove if Jesus of Nazareth is God or not. All we have to do is find out if He is a lunatic or a liar. If He is neither, He must be the Son of God" (Nee, 1997). C. S. Lewis in his 1942 book *Mere Christianity* gives his often quoted argument (Lewis, 2015). He says, first of all, we cannot just accept Jesus only as a great moral teacher, a good man who teaches us good things. We can't because that is not what Jesus claimed. Jesus claimed to be God! As C. S. Lewis states, because Jesus claims to be God, if He is not God: "He would be either a lunatic...or else he would be the devil from hell," a lunatic or a liar.

Let the reader be clear. You have to make the choice. You can either believe Jesus was a crazy man and should be locked up in an insane asylum, spit on Him or kill Him as a liar or demon...OR, as Lewis says: "you can fall at his feet and call him Lord and God"(Lewis, 2015).

Now it seems obvious that He was neither a lunatic nor a liar, so we have to come to the amazing and somewhat terrifying conclusion, especially if you are not saved, that He was and is God, just as He claimed. The reader is encouraged to look at all of the evidence of this book, the rest of the evidence in the Bible, the historical evidence and scientific support, and come to your own conclusion. It is this author's heartfelt hope that you also will make Him Lord of your life as millions upon millions have, including rich and poor, great leaders and thinkers, educated and ignorant, famous men and woman, simple and unknown. They have all accepted the free gift of grace purchased by the shedding of the blood of Jesus, God's blood. Repent of your sins and thank your God and Saviour for loving you so much that He would become man and suffer and die in your place to pay for your sins. And now He is preparing a place for His saints in heaven, where we will dwell in unfathomable joy with Him for eternity. And any man that comes to Him in repentance and faith will be in no wise cast out (John 6:37) and welcomed back to the Father and into eternal life in heaven.

Discussion Questions:

1. What did Machen say is another clear indication that Jesus claimed He was God? Explain.

2. According to the Scriptures, who is the source of eternal life? List one Scripture where Jesus says to believe in Himself.

3. Compare Psalm 100:3 to John 10:27. How does this support the deity of Christ?

4. What is Jesus Christ claiming He is in John 14:6? Compare to Psalm 86:11.

5. In John 8:19 and 14:7-9, what is Jesus claiming? Explain.

6. List three amazing things Jesus Christ claims about Himself in John 6:51-54. How does this support the deity of Christ?

7. Compare John 5:23 and John 17:5 with Isaiah 42:8. Jesus claims the honor and glory God reserves for Himself. Discuss.

V. Divine Birth, Life, Death, Resurrection, Ascension and Return

Another clear testimony to deity of Christ was etched on the canvass of His divine birth; His holy, sinless, supernatural life; His death; His resurrection; and His final ascension to the throne of God, as well as His heralded imminent return to earth.

Divine Birth

He started life as the incarnate God, supernaturally conceived (John 1:14). Isaiah 7:14 has been accepted as a messianic verse referring to Jesus among orthodox theologians and Christians over the centuries. It states: "Therefore the Lord himself shall give you a sign; Behold, a virgin shall conceive, and bear a son, and shall call his name Immanuel." There was consensus within the early church that Jesus' birth was like no other man's has been and like no other man's ever will be. He was miraculously born of a virgin and conceived by the Holy Spirit of God. In Matthew 1:18, the Bible states that Mary was found with child, espoused to Joseph but "before they came together."

And in Matthew 1:23, the New Testament Scripture refers to Isaiah 7:14 saying "Behold, a virgin shall be with child, and shall bring forth a son, and they shall call his name Emmanuel, which being interpreted is, God with us." And in Luke 1:27 Mary is again referred to as a virgin. And Mary herself testifies to this in verse 34. After the angel tells Mary she will conceive, she asks: "How shall this be, seeing I know not a man." To "know not" refers to not having had physical relations with a man. Christ was not like other men. He was God enrobed in flesh, fully God and fully man, born of a virgin, which is impossible within the limitations of mortal man. As the angel of God told Mary, that which is "conceived in her is of the Holy Ghost."

Divine Life (Ministry)

The divine life Christ led after birth testified to His deity. He lived a sinless life; he was impeccable (could not sin). "Orthodox theologians generally agree that Jesus Christ never committed any sin" (Walvoord, 1969). As Walvoord later states:

> "A proper doctrine of the impeccability of Christ therefore affirms the reality of the temptations of Christ due to the fact that He had a human nature which was temptable. If the human nature had been unsustained as in the case of Adam by the divine nature, it is clear that the human nature of Christ might have sinned. This possibility, however, is completely removed by the presence of the divine nature." (Walvoord, 1969, p. 149)

While Christ experienced temptation, it was without the possibility of yielding to it. He was fully man but also fully God. He had no human father and so did not have original sin. "Yet, in full experience of these longings, Christ was completely in control of Himself," Walvoord continues:

> "He could not sin. While the person of Christ could therefore be tempted, there was no possibility of sin

entering the life of Him appointed from eternity to be the spotless Lamb of God." (p. 152)

As the Scriptures relate in 2 Corinthians 5:21, "For he hath made him to be sin for us, who knew no sin; that we might be made the righteousness of God in him." In 1 Peter 2:22, speaking of Jesus, the Bible tells us, Jesus was one "Who did no sin, neither was guile found in his mouth." And Hebrews 4:15 states about Jesus: "but was in all points tempted like as we are, yet without sin." Christ was touched with the "feelings of our infirmities" but sinned not. Christ was impeccable.

The miracles He wrought testify to His deity. As Melito of Sardis wrote around 77 years after the death of the Apostle John:

> "The activities of Christ after his baptism, and especially his miracles, gave indication and assurance to the world of the deity hidden in his flesh." (Melito of Sardis, 177 AD)

Making a catalogue of all of the miracles Christ did is not within the scope of this primer. In fact, the Bible record in John 21:25 reveals:

> "And there are also many other things which Jesus did, the which, if they should be written every one, I suppose that even the world itself could not contain the books that should be written. Amen."

But certainly it would be critical for this primer to present them in broad relief. Jesus Christ our Lord defied the laws of science and turned water into wine (John 2:1-11). He healed the sick, gave sight to the blind, speech to the dumb, hearing to the deaf,

(Matthew 11:2-5, 15:30; Mark 1:31, 34; John 9:1-7) and He raised the dead (Luke 7:14-15, 8:54-55; John 5:25, 11:43-44). Christ had power over the nature and its laws in that He calmed the wind and the waves, withered trees with a word and walked on water (Mark 4:39-41, John 6:19-21). He knew where people were when He had not seen them (such as Nathanael, as recorded in John 1:48-49), and knew of people without being told about them (John 4:29). Jesus fed thousands with meals not sufficient for ten (Matthew 14:15-21, 15:32-38). Because of the miracles, "many believed in his name, when they saw the miracles which he did."

Divine Love of Christ

Jesus Christ our Lord's self-sacrificial life and love for humanity was beyond human comprehension or attainment and revealed in a very special way His equality with God (Philippians 2:6). For God is love. As is stated in Romans 5:6-8:

> "For when we were yet without strength, in due time Christ died for the ungodly. For scarcely for a righteous man will one die: yet peradventure for a good man some would even dare to die. But God commendeth his love toward us, in that, while we were yet sinners, Christ died for us."

As the Bible relates in 1 Peter 2:22-24, our Christ "who did no sin," "Who when he was reviled, reviled not again; when he suffered, he threatened not," "Who his own self bare our sins in his own body on the tree," gave His life willingly for the wicked souls of all men. This selfless Saviour was not forced to do it, to give His life, but as stated in John 10:18:

"No man taketh it from me, but I lay it down of myself. I have power to lay it down, and I have power to take it again. This commandment have I received of my Father."

Jesus gave His life freely, of His own choice. And in the midst of a humiliating, painful death, He exclaimed, "Father, if thou be willing, remove this cup from me: nevertheless not my will, but thine, be done" (Luke 22:42).

Jesus faced unimaginable brutality and humiliation, beaten until the flesh was ripped off His body, marred beyond recognition, buffeted, spit on and reviled, His beard plucked out, a crown of thorns pressed down on His head digging bloody furrows into His brow, nailed to a cross of crucifixion with metal posts hammered into His hands and feet. And, then, according to the Bible, He was punished as God unleashed the billows of His wrath for the sins of mankind on Messiah Jesus, and turned away from the Son who was clothed in the garment of our wicked sin so grievous to God (see Habakkuk 1:13). God separated Himself from His only begotten who was the eternal object of His eternal love. Jesus foreknew all of this prior to the actual events, and related it aforehand to the disciples, knowing what death He would die. Jesus still willingly went to His death. And, with a love incomprehensible to mortal man: "who for the joy that was set before him endured the cross, despising the shame, and is set down at the right hand of the throne of God" (Hebrews 12:2).

For the joy, you say? What joy? It is the joy of glorifying the Father, by laying down His life to save this perverse, sin-laden, ungrateful world. And as the wounded Saviour hung on the cross where we should have hung, after being mercilessly punished, humiliated and mocked, Jesus Christ our Lord looked upon those who had done this thing and exclaimed the inexplicable: "Father, forgive them; for they know not what they do" (Luke 23:34). This so great, supernatural love was expressed on the cross, our Saviour emptied Himself, the paschal lamb sacrificed to atone for our sins. This love can be nothing but divine.

Death

First, regarding Jesus Christ's supernatural death Walvoord states: "No event of time or eternity compares with the transcending significance of the death of Christ on the cross." (Walvoord, 1969) This event of amazing significance was accompanied by many observable supernatural events. After Jesus had uttered His final words and "gave up the ghost" (Luke 23:46):

- "Now from the sixth hour there was darkness over all the land unto the ninth hour." (Matthew 27:45)
- "The veil of the temple was rent in twain from the top to the bottom" (Matthew 27:51). Estimates are that the veil was as much as seven inches thick.
- "The earth did quake" (Matthew 27:51)
- "The rock rent" (Split into pieces; Matthew 27:51)
- "The graves were opened" (Matthew 27:52)

The veil of the Temple separated the Holy of Holies where the Ark of the Covenant was and where God would come down between the wings of the Cherubim, an awesome and fearful event for God's chosen people Israel. Only the High Priest could enter the Holy of Holies, and only once a year, and only with blood. However, the separation of God and man was forever overcome by the atoning sacrifice of the Lamb of God,

High priest, Saviour and Holy God, who shed His blood once and for all, making God's presence accessible to all saints and repentant sinners at all times. As it says in Hebrews 10:20:

> "Having therefore, brethren, boldness to enter into the holiest by the blood of Jesus, by a new and living way, which he hath consecrated for us, through the veil, that is to say, his flesh."

As stated above, at His death there were earthquakes and the rocks themselves split in two. This happened in the Old Testament on a number of occasion related to the God (see 1 Kings 19:11, Numbers 16:32). And there were witnesses to these events. The centurion who was watching Jesus greatly feared when he saw the earthquake. and exclaimed: "Truly this was the Son of God." And the dead arose from their graves. Ezekiel 37:13 states, "Ye shall know that I am the LORD, when I have opened your graves." In John 5:21 it is written: "For as the Father raiseth up the dead, and quickeneth them; even so the Son quickeneth whom he will." And after His resurrection, these resurrected people appeared to many (Matthew 27:53). Truly the death of Jesus Christ our Lord was a divine event of supernatural significance and bore the mark of God Almighty.

Resurrection

Christ's resurrection from the dead testifies to His deity. In 1 Corinthians 15:1-8, Paul relates how the Resurrection was witnessed by Cephas (Peter), then the twelve apostles, then by 500 brethren "at once," then James, then all the apostles together and lastly by Paul. In support of this claim he states that many of the more than 500 witnesses were still alive, implying that the supernatural event could be attested to by "first hand witnesses." In fact the Bible recounts at least ten times in the four Gospels that Jesus appeared to His followers after His resurrection. The final time was in Acts 1:8-9 during which He commissioned His followers to be witnesses of the gospel in all the world after which He ascended to the Father in heaven. Acts 1:3 states clearly:

> "To whom also he shewed himself alive after his passion by many infallible proofs, being seen of them forty days, and speaking of the things pertaining to the kingdom of God."

Jesus prophesied of His own resurrection in John 2:19. And in Matthew 12:40 Christ Jesus says, "For as Jonas was three days and three nights in the whale's belly; so shall the Son of man be three days and three nights in the heart of the earth." Truly Jesus' prophetic utterances, and the fulfillment through His bodily resurrection give another clear indication of the deity of Christ. It was this resurrection that surely sealed our redemption:

> "But if there be no resurrection of the dead, then is Christ not risen; And if Christ be not risen, then is our preaching vain, and your faith is also vain." (1 Corinthians 15:13-14)

Jesus' resurrection was prophesied, was supernaturally performed and, to His glory and our blessing, it seals the promise of our hope of redemption.

Ascension

And, finally, His ascension gives further support for the claim of the deity of Christ (2 Timothy 4:1). After Christ had appeared for the last time unto the apostles, Jesus Christ our

Lord "was taken up; and a cloud received him out of their sight" (Acts 1:9). As the apostles watched and looked upward toward where Jesus ascended, the angels said, "this same Jesus, which is taken up from you into heaven, shall so come in like manner as ye have seen him go into heaven." Christ predicted His ascension and return during his earthly ministry (John 14:3) before His resurrection from the dead. Christ also predicted His ascension after His resurrection (John 20:17). As Walvoord states: "The ascension is the important link between His work on earth and His work in heaven which begins with the ascension" (Walvoord, 1969).

Jesus' ascension was prophesied and verified, the apostles witnessing it in the first chapter of Acts. In heaven He is firstly exalted: "Therefore being by the right hand of God exalted" (Acts 2:33, Philippians 2:9). Christ is exalted and given "a name which is above every name," at which "every knee should bow, of things in heaven, and things in earth, and things under the earth" (Philippians 2:10). Secondly, He sits at the right hand of power (Mark 14:62). And all power is given to Him "in heaven and in earth" (Matthew 28:18). The ascended Christ is then to be exalted above all things, worshipped by all things, and given power over all things. This can only be true of the divine, God "Almighty."

Finally, the ascended Christ makes "intercession for the transgressors" (Isaiah 53:12), for us.

> "Who is he that condemneth? It is Christ that died, yea rather, that is risen again, who is even at the right hand of God, who also maketh intercession for us." (Romans 8:34)

It is so characteristic of God's extravagant love that Jesus, our God, is pitiful and merciful to the insignificant, with an amazing love, condescending to intercede, to plead for us as our advocate in heaven!

Imminent Return

Implications, types and prophecies of end times events and the return of Christ are pictured in the Old and New Testaments in many books. Although this author holds to a pre-millennial, pre-tribulation view of end times prophecy, the goal of this book is not to settle the debate on the design or chronology of end times events but to make an incontestable claim for the deity of Christ. Suffice it to say here that accounts alluding to Christ's return in the Bible, whether *for* His church to meet them in the air or the second coming to earth *with* His church to set up His millennial Kingdom, describe supernatural occurrences. And Jesus is depicted as the central, deified figure and focus, and the events as of a powerful and supernatural nature. This chapter will briefly cover a few of the descriptions of these events to make the point that descriptions of the return of Christ in the Bible unabashedly support claims that Christ is, was, and will ever be our great God and Saviour.

For example, those who hold to the pre-tribulational view believe that the Scripture reveals in 1 Thessalonians 4:15-18 that Christ will first come to catch away His church prior to the coming seven-year Tribulation. As it says in 1 Thessalonians, "the dead in Christ shall rise first" and then "we which are alive and remain shall be caught up together with them in the clouds to meet the Lord in the air." The Greek word *harpazo* is used here for the English word "caught up," and means to seize or catch away or to claim for oneself.

When Christ appears in the heavens to catch away His church, it will be "with a shout, with the voice of the archangel, and with the trump of God" (1 Thessalonians 4:16). So Jesus' coming will be announced by the archangel. This word "archangel" does not appear anywhere else in the New Testament and "properly means chief angel" (Barnes, 1983). And then the "trump of God." Trumpets were used by Israel to announce feasts and religious occasion or warnings. But this is the "trump of God," a very ominous sign. In Exodus 19:16, when Israel had left Egypt and was encamped before Mount Sinai, God descended with thunder and lightning to meet the people. A trump from God sounded "exceeding loud, so that all the people that was in the camp trembled." So the voice of the archangel and the trump of God were used here to herald an ominous event of divine proportions, the return of Christ for His church.

As Jesus returns for His followers, His church will be caught up into the air to be with Him forever. Let the reader note that those who rise first are referred to as the "dead in Christ"; they are Jesus Christ's, His dead, His purchased possessions, as are all believers. And all of this will happen "in a moment, in the twinkling of an eye, at the last trump" and "we shall be changed" (1 Corinthians 15:52-55). During that infinitesimal flash of time, "this corruptible must put on incorruption, and this mortal must put on immortality", and we are given new immortal bodies "to die no more" (Clarke, 1977). And Jesus is seen as the source of power and central figure of this divine spectacle.

Many scholars argue that Matthew 24:29-34 describes the second coming of Christ. In verse 29 the Bible says "Immediately after the tribulation of those days." Whether you believe this describes the rapture or the second coming, in verse 30 Jesus describes His return in this way: "And then shall appear the sign of the Son of man in heaven: and then shall all the tribes of the earth mourn, and they shall see the Son of man coming in the clouds of heaven with power and great glory." So there will be a sign of Jesus in heaven, and all the earth will mourn, and Jesus will come with "power" and "glory," as a divine King. Verse 31 tells us that Jesus will send *His* angels to gather *His* elect "from the four winds, and from one end of heaven to the other." Note again, they are *His* angels. Angels are heavenly beings created by God to serve and minister to Him. But Jesus here is given identical authority over these heavenly beings. In Revelation they are also depicted as Jesus' angels. And the saints of God, all who are saved, are portrayed as being the elect of Jesus, His elect. This clearly presents Jesus as resurrected from the dead and bearing the glory, honor, power, and authority of God Himself.

There are so many other relevant descriptions of the return of Jesus in other books of the Bible, but this should be sufficient to make the point that the return of Christ will be a divine event in which Jesus will be honored as ruler and God of all creation. In Revelation 21 the Bible says that, in the end of times, in the New Jerusalem, the city will have "no need of the sun, neither of the moon, to shine in it for the glory of God did lighten it, and the Lamb, is the light thereof." The Lamb is Jesus, and He at the end of time will, as deity, share being our light with God the Father for eternity.

Discussion Questions:

1. Explain why Christ's birth was like no man's birth and was supernatural. List Scriptures to support.
2. Discuss why Jesus Christ's life was divine, like God. Please discuss His sinlessness and miracles. List Scriptures to support.
3. Discuss the death of our Lord Jesus and why it supports His deity. List Scriptures to support. Discuss in detail the events that happened at His death and how they support the claim that He is God.
4. Discuss the resurrection of our Lord Jesus and why it supports His deity. List Scriptures to support including prophecies of His resurrection.
5. Discuss the evidence and witnesses, listing Scripture, of Jesus' resurrection.
6. Discuss the ascension of our Lord Jesus and why it supports His deity. List Scriptures to support, including prophesy within Scripture.
7. Discuss the return of our Lord Jesus and why it supports that Jesus in Jehovah God. List Scriptures to support, including prophecy within Scripture.

VI. Jesus' Divine Attributes:

The gospel clearly and unambiguously proclaims that Jesus Christ shared divine attributes with Jehovah God.

Holy

In Leviticus 21:8 the Lord God says, "for I the LORD, which sanctify you, am holy." Psalm 145:17 states, "The LORD is righteous in all his ways, and holy in all his works." God's supreme attribute, from which all other attributes find their source, is holiness. Leviticus 19:2 reads, "Ye shall be holy: for I the LORD your God am Holy." First Peter 1:16 reiterates this, when speaking of God: "Because it is written, Be ye holy, for I am holy."

In the Hebrew the word used for holy is *Qadowsh* and in the Greek *hagios*. Both these words similarly are defined as "sacred, set apart." Webster's 1828 dictionary defines holy as "Perfect in a moral sense, free of sin and sinful affections, perfectly just and good" (Webster's, 1967). God is always love, just, merciful, kind. He is separate from all sin.

Referring to Jesus, Hebrews 7:26 says: "For such an high priest became us, who is holy, harmless, undefiled, separate from sinners, and made higher than the heavens." In Mark 1:24 Jesus crosses paths with an unclean spirit, a possessed man. When he recognized Jesus the spirit cried out, "I know who thou art, the Holy One of God." And in Acts 3 Peter preached a seminal sermon to the unbelieving Jews. He confronted them, saying in verse 14, "But ye denied the Holy One and the Just, and desired a murderer to be granted unto you." And then Peter upbraided them for having "killed the Prince of life, whom God hath raised from the dead; whereof ye are witnesses."

The Bible is clear. As God is Holy, Jesus is Holy. Jesus, as we said earlier, knew no sin, did no sin, and was without sin. Jesus was separate from sinners. He could not be an acceptable sacrifice for your and my sin if He weren't holy. He was the Holy Lamb of God sacrificed for our sin that we might live. His cross at Golgotha became a massive brazen altar on which our Jesus, God incarnate, was crucified to pay the price for our redemption. He is Holy and undefiled and separate from sinners. He is the God-man who is the Son of God and God the Son.

Omnipresent

In Scripture Jesus is declared to be omnipresent [all-present]. McDowell and Larson write:

> "Just as God is omnipresent in a personal sense, and thus is able to help, deliver, love, defend, and meet His people's deepest longings and needs, so the New Testament describes Christ also as omnipresent." (McDowell & Larson, 1983)

When speaking of Jehovah in Psalm 139:7, the Old Testament declares, "whither shall I go from thy spirit? Or whither shall I flee from thy presence?" It then goes on to state that the Lord Jehovah is in heaven and in hell, and in the uttermost parts of the sea. God is everywhere. In John 3:13 the Bible states, "And no man hath ascended up to heaven, but he that came down from heaven, even the Son of man which is in heaven." So Jesus is in both places, on earth and in heaven. In Matthew

18:20 Jesus says, "For where two or three are gathered together in my name, there am I in the midst of them." Jesus Christ also dwells in the hearts of every saved saint of God. In John 8:58 Jesus states, "Verily, verily, I say unto you, Before Abraham was, I am." He took the title given to God, and one that expresses God's presence outside of time, omnipresent in a temporal sense. Christ was omnipresent physically (on earth and in heaven), spiritually (there am I in the midst of them) as well as temporally (even unto the end).

Omniscience

Jesus Christ also shares the Divine attribute of omniscience (all-knowing) with God. Psalm 139:1 states of Jehovah God, "O LORD, thou hast searched me, and known me" and later in verse 4, "For there is not a word in my tongue, but, lo, O Lord, thou knowest it altogether." First Kings 8:39, speaking of Lord Jehovah God, says: "for thou, even thou only, knowest the hearts of all the children of men."

But Jesus also "knew all men" and "what was in man," which only an omniscient God could know (John 2:24-25). In John 21:17 Peter says of Jesus, "And he said unto him, Lord, thou knowest all things." As R. A. Torrey (2004) points out:

- Jesus knows the secret lives of people, as He did the Samaritan woman at the well, for nothing is hidden from Him (John 4:16-19).
- Jesus knows the secret thoughts of people (Mark 2:8). In Luke 5:22 "Jesus perceived their thoughts," the thoughts of the scribes and Pharisees. As explained above, Jesus knew/knows all men and what "is in man" (John 2:24-25).

- Jesus knew what men were doing in places where He wasn't located when it happened. For example, Nathaniel calls Him "the son of God" because Jesus knew Nathaniel's personality (no guile) without ever having met him and remarked that He saw Nathaniel under a fig tree when Jesus hadn't been physically in that place (John 1:47-49). He also knew who were unbelievers and who would betray Him.

- Jesus knew the future (John 16). And as a result of what Jesus says in verse 30, His disciples exclaimed, "Now are we sure that thou knowest all things" and, "we believe that thou camest forth from God." (Also see John 13:1, Luke 5:4-6.)

- In Jesus are hidden all the treasures of wisdom and knowledge (Colossians 2:3).

It was by His power of omniscience that Jesus Christ our Lord made Himself known to the disciples in the beginning of the His ministry and after He had risen from the dead. It was in Luke 5:4-10, at the beginning of His ministry, that He entered the ship of Simon and asked him to cast his net on the right side of the boat and they caught "a great multitude of fishes." And Peter worshipped Him. It was in John 21:6, at the end of His ministry as the resurrected Saviour, that Jesus on the shore at the sea of Tiberias asked the disciples in their boat to cast their nets on the right side, and they once again caught a "multitude of fishes." In both cases the disciples had labored fishing all night with no success. But Jesus knew and He knew them. He knew all things that were to follow, for He is God.

Omnipotence

Jesus not only shares omnipresence and omniscience with God but also omnipotence (all-powerful). As Walvoord relates, "The evidence for the omnipotence of Christ is as decisive as proof for other attributes." Sometimes it takes the form of physical power, but more often it refers to authority over creation" (Walvoord, 1969, p. 29). Here is scriptural support for various expressions of His omnipotence:

- He has the power to forgive sins (Matthew 9:6)
- He has all power in heaven and earth (Matthew 28:18)
- He has power over nature (Luke 8:25)
- He has power to raise the dead (Luke 7:14-15, 8:54-55; John 5:25, 11:43-44)
- He has power over His own life and to raise Himself from the dead (John 2:19, 10:18)
- He has power to give eternal life to others (John 10:28, 17:2) and to transform their bodies (Philippians 3:21, 1 Corinthians 15:52-57)
- He has power to heal physically and cast out demons (Mark 1:29-34)
- He has power over demonic forces (Matthew 8:16; Luke 4:33-36, 8:30-33)

Jesus speaks of these powers as residing in His person. In Matthew 28:18 Jesus states, "All power is given unto me in heaven and in earth." He claims the power as His own. When speaking of His power He uses the terms "I," "me," and "my." For example, in Luke 10:19 Jesus says: "Behold, I give unto you power" and the disciples had joy because the devils were subject to them "through thy name." He said He gives them power. And in John 10:9, Jesus declares, "I am the door: by me if any man enter in, he shall be saved." Jesus is claiming that He is the key to salvation—directly, not as an intermediary, but as the primary cause of salvation. However this power is reserved for God in the Old Testament (Isaiah 43:11, 45:22). It is through Him and to whom He chooses that the Father is revealed (Luke 10:22). No one can know God but through Him. In Mark 16:17-18, Jesus sent the disciples into all the world, attended by powers that were, in Jesus' words, "In my name." In His commission in Luke, He states, "thus it is written" that "repentance and remission of sins should be preached in his name," in the name of Christ (Luke 24:47).

Pre-Existent/Eternal

As God is pre-existent, so is Jesus Christ. Psalm 90:2 presents God as existing prior to Creation. Genesis 1 declares God was in the beginning and "created the heaven and the earth." Proverbs 8:23 states, "I was set up from everlasting, from the beginning, or ever the earth was." At the same time in John 17:5, Jesus claims He had glory "before the world was." Speaking of Jesus, in John 1:1 the Bible states, "The same was in the beginning with God." In Colossians 1:17 Christ "is before all things and by him all things consist." Therefore, Christ is as God in His pre-existence.

Christ is God in His eternality. In Deuteronomy 33:27 God as "Elohim" is referred to as: "The eternal God is thy refuge." Isaiah 40:28 says:

> "Hast thou not known? Hast thou not heard, that the everlasting God, the LORD, the Creator of the ends of the earth, fainteth not, neither is weary? There is no searching of his understanding."

65

Referring in this verse to Jehovah, the word used in the Hebrew for "everlasting" is *owlam* which is defined as continuous, perpetual, eternal. Again in Genesis 21:33 Jehovah God is referred to as "the everlasting God." And Psalm 90:2 proclaims: "even from everlasting to everlasting, thou art God."

In the same way, Jesus is referred to as eternal. In Isaiah 9:6, a classic prophetic passage referring to the Lord Jesus, the Bible states:

> "For unto us a child is born, unto us a son is given: and the government shall be upon his shoulder: and his name shall be called Wonderful, Counsellor, The mighty God, The everlasting Father, The Prince of Peace."

Here Jesus is the "everlasting Father." In another prophetic passage, Micah 5:2, discussing the birthplace of the Messiah in Bethlehem, the coming Christ is referred to as one whose "goings forth have been from of old, from everlasting." John 17:24 Jesus speaks of God's eternal love for the eternal Son: "for thou lovest me before the foundation of the world." And in Hebrews Jesus is referred to as "the same yesterday, and today, and forever" (Hebrews 13:8).

Finally, in Revelation 1:8, the Lord God, using the Greek word *Kurios*, is referred to as "Alpha and Omega, the beginning and the ending,...which was, and which is to come, the Almighty." But later, in Revelation 1:11, the Son is given the name of "Alpha and Omega," "the first and the last." And in Revelation 1:18, Jesus, who is referred to as "like unto the Son of man," says:

"I am he that liveth, and was dead; and, behold, I am alive for evermore, Amen; and have the keys of hell and of death."

Jesus shares eternality with eternal God.

Immutable

Jesus is immutable as God is immutable (unchangeable). In Malachi 3:6 the Lord God states emphatically, "For I am the LORD, I change not; therefore ye sons of Jacob are not consumed." In James 1:17 we find "Every good gift and every perfect gift is from above, and cometh down from the Father of lights, with whom is no variableness, neither shadow of turning." There is no variableness or turning for God. In Job 23:13 we find "But he is in one mind, and who can turn him? and what his soul desireth, even that he doeth." In Malachi 3:6 the Scripture relates: "For I am the LORD, I change not". Jesus is also immutable as God is, for Jesus is "the same yesterday, and today, and forever" (Hebrews 13:8). Immutability is then another divine trait shared between our Holy God and the "God with us," Jesus Christ the Lord.

Object of Honor and Worship

As God is to be, Christ is to be the object of honor and worship. The First Commandment reads: "Thou shalt have no other gods before me" (Exodus 20:3). Nor are we to make any graven image or to bow down to and worship any other gods beside Jehovah God. The Lord our God is one Lord (Deuteronomy 6:4, Mark 12:29). In Matthew 4:10 Jesus says: "Thou shalt worship the Lord thy God, and him only shalt thou serve." Exodus 34:14 clearly contents: "For thou shalt worship no other god: for the LORD, whose name is Jealous, is a jealous God." In Revelation 22:9 when John fell down at the feet of the angel and worshipped him, the angel said, "See thou do it not" and further admonished John to "worship God" instead. And in Acts 10:26, when Cornelius fell down at Peter's feet and worshipped him, Peter stood him up and reminded him, "I myself also am a man." God, and only God, is to be the object of our worship.

It is interesting, as Robinson explains, that Paul prayed to Jesus 25 times (Robinson, 1949, p. 134). In Hebrews 1:6, God Himself states, "And again, when he bringeth in the firstbegotten into the world, he saith, And let all the angels of God worship him." God Himself, who is the voice in the preceding verses, directs all the angels to worship Jesus Christ. People also worshipped Christ Jesus. In Matthew 2:11, the wise men worshipped the Christ child. In Matthew 8:2, the leper worshipped Jesus. In John 9:38, the blind man whose sight was restored worshipped Jesus. And in Mark 5:6, the demoniac worshipped Jesus. In Revelation 5:12 the angels worships the Lamb (Jesus) who is worthy and "slain to receive power, and riches, and wisdom, and strength, and honour, and glory, and blessing."

The Word of God makes it clear that Jesus is worthy of the identical form of worship as is God. In Romans 14:11, the Bible states: "As I live saith the Lord, every knee shall bow to me, and every tongue shall confess to God." In verses 3-8, the Word of God uses "Lord" and "God" interchangeably. And Romans 14:11 is a parallel verse to Isaiah 45:23. Isaiah 45:21 uses LORD (Jehovah) and God (Elohim) interchangeably also, as is done in Romans 14. God is the LORD and the LORD is God. The verse finishes with "there is none beside me." In verse 22, God declares, "Look unto me, and be ye saved, all the ends of the earth for I am God, and there is none else" (see

Acts 4:12). There is no confusion that in Isaiah 45 God (and God alone) is to be worshipped, and given the title of LORD.

So only God is to be the object of our worship. However, as further confirmation of Jesus Christ's divine nature, in a parallel verse in Philippians 2:10, the Word of God declares, "That at the name of Jesus every knee should bow, of things in heaven, and things in earth, and things under the earth; And that every tongue should confess that Jesus Christ is Lord, to the glory of God the Father." In other words, everything in all existence is commanded by God to bow the knee and confess with the tongue the Lord Jesus, the identical language the Bible uses in Romans 14 and in Isaiah 45 which, in Isaiah, is clearly designated to apply to God and God alone. In this passage in Philippians 2, God commands all creation to worship Jesus, to declare Jesus Christ as Lord; a term used both in Romans and Isaiah for Jehovah God. This is an indisputable declaration of the deity of Jesus Christ our Lord. Also note that the Greek term used for "Lord," as applied to Jesus in Philippians 2:10, is the Greek word *kurios*, the same term used over and over again in Romans 14 for God.

And at no time did Jesus ever warn them or chastise anyone for worshipping Him. The disciples even worshipped Him. When they saw the risen Christ in Matthew 28:17, "they worshipped him." Again, in Luke 24:52 the Word of God states that "they worshipped him," the risen Christ. As Warfield points out, "Christianity is pre-eminently the worship of Christ" (Warfield, 1929, p. 372).

Forgives Sin

According to the Bible, God forgives sin as Christ forgives sin. Isaiah 55:7 states:

69

"Let the wicked forsake his way, and the unrighteous man his thoughts: and let him return unto the LORD, and he will have mercy upon him; and to our God, for he will abundantly pardon."

Jeremiah 31:34 declares:

"And they shall teach no more every man his neighbour, and every man his brother, saying, Know the LORD: for they shall all know me, from the least of them unto the greatest of them, saith the LORD: for I will forgive their iniquity, and I will remember their sin no more."

In 2 Chronicles 7:14 it is written:

"If my people, which are called by my name, shall humble themselves, and pray, and seek my face, and turn from their wicked ways; then will I hear from heaven, and will forgive their sin, and will heal their land."

As Tertullian says: "God alone is without sin. The only man without sin is Christ; for Christ is also God" (Tertullian, c. 215 AD). Only the sinless one can forgive sin, and Jesus Christ as God forgives sins. When Jesus healed the man let down through the roof in Luke 5:20, He said: "thy sins are forgiven thee." But when the scribes and Pharisees heard this they "began to reason, saying, Who is this which speaketh blasphemies? Who can forgive sins, but God alone?" (Luke 5:21; see also Mark 2:7).

In Matthew 9:6, Jesus Himself claims the "power on earth to forgive sins." "Repentance and remission of sins should be preached in his [Jesus'] name." When Jesus was in the house of Simon, He said to a woman who was a well-known sinner, "Thy sins are forgiven" (Luke 7:48). In Colossians 2:13, speaking of Jesus, Paul teaches that: "And you, being dead in your sins and the uncircumcision of your flesh, hath he quickened together with him, having forgiven you all trespasses." There is no question that the biblical record shows that only God can forgive sins, and that Jesus, as God, has the power to and did forgive sins.

Jesus Has the Keys to Heaven and Hell

God and Jesus both have the power to send people to eternal damnation and hell. We find written in Matthew 10:28, "And fear not them which kill the body, but are not able to kill the soul: but rather fear him which is able to destroy both soul and body in hell." That is, fear God who has this power. In Psalm 9:17, the Bible states: "The wicked shall be turned into hell, and all the nations that forget God." Ezekiel 31:16 reads:

> "I made the nations to shake at the sound of his fall, when I cast him down to hell with them that descend into the pit: and all the trees of Eden, the choice and best of Lebanon, all that drink water, shall be comforted in the nether parts of the earth."

The Bible tells us in Revelation 1:18 that Jesus Christ also has the keys to heaven and hell. In Matthew 25:31 and 33, Jesus Christ, referring to Himself, says: "When the Son of man shall come in his glory," He will "set the sheep on his right hand, but the goats on his left." And in verse 41, "Then shall he say also unto them on the left hand, Depart from me, ye cursed, into everlasting fire, prepared for the devil and his angels."

71

Those who did wickedly in this life He shall condemn to "everlasting punishment."

Compare this to Matthew 7:21-23, where Jesus states that: "Many will say to me in that day, Lord, Lord, have we not prophesied in thy name? and in thy name have cast out devils? and in thy name done many wonderful works?" Then Jesus will profess to them, "I never knew you: depart from me, ye that work iniquity." As spiritual death is in essence separation from God, so the consequence for unregenerate man is to depart from Christ into everlasting punishment.

And in Revelation 21:27, only those "which are written in the Lamb's book of life," Jesus' book of life, shall enter into heaven. All others will be "cast into the lake of fire" (Revelation 20:15). Therefore those that know not God will reap the wrath of God the Son who has the keys to heaven and hell.

Salvation and Eternal Life through Jesus

Jesus Himself is identified as one who has the power to grant salvation and eternal life, an attribute only God can have, and not a mortal man. That only God can have this power is only reasonable and is established in the Old Testament. It is unreasonable to think that a mortal can grant immortality. In Isaiah 45:22, God says, "Look unto me, and be ye saved, all the ends of the earth: For I am God, and there is none else." In Acts 2:21, the Scripture reveals: "And it shall come to pass, that whosoever shall call on the name of the Lord shall be saved." In a parallel verse in Joel 2:32, God's Word says, "And it shall come to pass, that whosoever shall call on the name of the LORD shall be delivered." This "LORD" is translated as the Lord Jehovah. Salvation and eternal life are of the Lord God.

Yet the Bible clearly establishes that Jesus Christ the Lord grants eternal life. In Acts 4:12, in a sermon preached by Peter to the rulers, elders, scribes, as well as others, he said of Jesus:

> "Neither is their salvation in any other: for there is none other name under heaven given among men, whereby we must be saved."

In Acts 16:31 the Bible states clearly, "Believe on the Lord Jesus Christ, and thou shalt be saved, and thy house." In Romans 1:16, Paul states that the gospel of Christ is "the power of God unto salvation." In John 3:36, those who believe on the Son receive everlasting life, and those who do not believe receive the wrath of God. Clearly Christ is a name by which salvation is received, and who has the power to grant eternal life, both divine attributes reserved for Jehovah God. Finally, in John 10:28 Jesus tells us, "And I give unto them eternal life; and they shall never perish." Jesus is the author of salvation and the source of eternal life. He is God.

Discussion Questions:

1. Discuss Jesus' holiness, omnipotence, omnipresence, and omniscience. Support each with Scripture. Discuss how each one is an attribute of God and how this supports the deity of Christ.

2. Discuss Jesus' pre-existence/eternality and immutability. Support each with Scripture. Discuss how each one is an attribute of God and how this supports the deity of Christ.

3. Discuss Exodus 20:3-4 and Isaiah 45:18, 21. Do these say that there is only one God and only He should be worshipped? Discuss the evidence in the New Testament that Jesus was worshipped. How does this support the deity of Christ?

4. Compare Isaiah 45:22-23, Romans 14:11, and Philippians 2:9-11. Show how God asks us to give the same glory and honor to Christ as God demands for Himself.

5. Show how in the Old and in the New Testament the Bible clearly states that only God can forgive sins. Did Jesus claim to be able to forgive sins? Support each answer with Scripture.

6. Who has the keys to heaven and hell? Discuss in terms of the deity of Christ.

7. Does Jesus have the power to grant salvation and eternal life? Explain. Support with Scripture.

VII. Consensus within the Early Church on the Deity of Christ

For early writers within the Christian church, the deity of Christ was not a question to be answered but a doctrinal assumption. As William Childs Robinson points out, the church from the very beginning was convinced that Christ was God incarnate (Robinson, 1949, p. 66). Christianity was basically from its roots founded upon the worship of Jesus Christ our Lord.

In an earlier research, this author examined a number of orthodox creeds, confessions, and catechisms to try to identify a body of biblical, consistent, uniform, fundamental, Christian doctrines that spanned the ages from the early church through to the modern era. One of the key doctrines, never questioned within the body of these fundamental documents, was the deity of Jesus Christ our Lord. In fact, many of the early creeds were reactions to doctrinal heresy, attempts to clearly quash the voice of those who supported these departures from early church fundamental doctrines. For example, one such heresy was Arianism (around AD 320), named after Arius Alexander, who denied the deity of Christ and claimed that the Son of God, Jesus, was a created being. The First Council of Nicaea condemned Arius in AD 325. The work of the Council resulted in the Nicene Creed, which proposed a clear statement as to the biblical basis for the deity of Christ. The Nicene Creed states in its second paragraph:

"And in one Lord Jesus Christ, the only begotten Son of God, begotten of the Father before all worlds; God of God, Light of Light, very God of very God; begotten, not made, being of one substance with the Father, by whom all things were made." (First Council of Nicea, c. 325 AD)

The overwhelming consensus of early Christian church leaders was that Christ, *Logos* (the Word), was clearly *Theos* (God). In fact, much of the writings coming out of the early church amounted to a call to arms against heretics who attacked the deity of Christ. The arguments were impassioned, and without fail unabashedly proclaiming the revealed Truth of the Bible, that Jesus Christ is God. Below are the testimonies of a number of these earlier Christians—most well-known theologians, priests, and scholars—dating from just before the death of the Apostle John until the late 4th century AD. Many of them have been given the honor of being called Early Church Fathers.

At the end of the first century, sometime prior to John's death, Clement of Rome, in his *Second Epistle to the Corinthians* states, "Brethren, we ought so to think of Jesus Christ as of God: as of the judge of the living and the dead" (Clement of Rome, c. 92-99 AD). During approximately the same time Ignatius, Bishop of Antioch, who is believed to have been a disciple of the Apostle John, in his *Epistle to the Trallians*, wrote, "Continue inseparable from Jesus Christ our God" (Ignatius, Bishop of Antioch, c. 110 AD). In his *Epistle to the Ephesians* he wrote of Jesus, "God Himself appearing in the form of a man, for the renewal of eternal life" (Ignatius, Bishop of Antioch, c. 110 AD). Theophilus, a later Bishop of Antioch, wrote, "For the divine writing itself teaches us that Adam said that he had heard the voice but what else is this voice but the word of God, who is also his Son." (Theophilus, c. 160 AD) Another interesting early church document was a letter from

Mathetes, being interpreted as an anonymous "disciple," to a pagan, Diognetius. He wrote, "as a king sends his Son, who is also king, so sent he him, as God he sent him; as men he sent him; as Saviour he sent him."

Justin Martyr, a child of two Greek pagan parents, studied rhetoric, poetry, history, and various schools of Greek philosophy. He was impressed with the zeal and steadfastness of Christian martyrs. By God's providence he met with an aged Christian man who shared his testimony of Christ, and "a flame" was kindled in his soul, and he became a Christian. He was eventually tried and beheaded for refusing to renounce his Christian faith. In his *Dialogue with Tropho* he stated: "For Christ is King, and Priest, and God and Lord...He preexisted as the Son of the Creator of things, being God, and that He was born a man by the Virgin" (Martyr, 140 AD). Tatian was a pupil of Justin Martyr who came to Rome from Syria and was converted to Christianity. In his impassioned address to Greek pagans he wrote, "We are not playing the fool, you Greeks, nor do we talk nonsense, when we report that God was born in the form of a man" (Tatian, 1970).

In the latter half of the 2nd century, although exact dating is somewhat problematic, there are a number of important apologetic documents by earlier church writers written to counter various heresies in the church, especially Gnosticism. Irenaeus, who eventually became Bishop of Lyons, was a convert to Christianity who had heard the teachings of Polycarp, who himself had heard the preaching of the Apostle John. His important work was *Refutation of Heresies*, in which he defended orthodox Christianity against its gnostic rivals (Irenaeus, c. 200 AD). In his words: "Christ Jesus, our Lord, and God, and Saviour, and King" and also:

"But he is himself in his own right, beyond all men who ever lived, God, Lord, and king eternal, and the incarnate word, proclaimed by all the prophets, the apostles...The Scriptures would not have borne witness to these things concerning Him, if, like everyone else, He were mere man."

Hippolytus was a late 2nd century scholar and apologist, whose best-known work was also crafted to expose the inaccuracy of the gnostic heresy. He wrote:

"For Christ is the God above all...He who is over all is God; for thus He speaks boldly, 'All things are delivered unto me of my Father.' He who is over all, God blessed, has been born; and having been made man, He is (yet) God for ever...And well has he named Christ the Almighty." (Roberts & Donaldson, Eds., 1994)

Clement of Alexandria, just as Justin Martyr, was the son of Greek pagans. He was a scholar and writer converted to Christianity by his last teacher, Pantaenus. He also wrote to counter the gnostic heresy that salvation could be achieved by esoteric knowledge. In his *Exhortation to the Greeks*, he writes:

"The Word, then, the Christ, is the cause both of our ancient beginning, for he was in God, and of our well-being. And now this same Word has appeared as man. He alone is both God and man, and the source of all our good things." (Martyr, 190 AD)

Therefore Clement of Alexandria clearly supports other writers in the early Christian church supporting the deity of Christ.

There were a number of notable contributors to the Christian writing during the 3rd and 4th centuries, also confirming the deity of Christ. Novatian was an early 3rd century scholar, priest, and theologian. He wrote:

> "For Scripture as much announces Christ as also God, as it announces God Himself as man. It has as much described Jesus Christ to be man, as moreover it has also described Christ the Lord to be God." (Novatian, 235 AD)

Tertullian was an author, somewhere around 200 AD, who lived in the ancient city of Carthage. He was known for being the first Christian writer to write in Latin; he wrote many seminal, brilliant works. Tertullian said, "The origins of both his substances display him as man and as God: from the one, born, and from the other, not born." He continues, "Yet we have never given vent to the phrases 'two Gods', or 'two Lords': not that it is untrue the Father is God, the Son is God, the Spirit is God, each is God" (Tertullian, c. 215 AD).

Arnobius, a vigorous apologist against the heathen, during the reign of Diocletian, in the 4th century, wrote a work entitled *Against the Pagans*. Similar to others, this work was a direct attack on heathen heresy, and an attempt to establish doctrinal orthodoxy. In it he set forth:

> "You worship, says my opponent, one who was born a mere human being. Even if that were true, as has been already said in former passages, yet, in consideration of the many liberal gifts which He has bestowed on us, He ought to be called and be

addressed as God. But since He is God in reality and without any shadow of doubt." (Arnobius, 305 AD)

Athanasius is the final of these early church writers covered here. He is notable as he was author of the Athanasian Creed. The Athanasian Creed is the seminal creed supporting the doctrine of the Trinity. In The Athanasian Creed, Athanasius wrote, "Just as the Father is he that is, so also his Word is one that is and is God over all" (Athanasius, 1951). This is another very clear affirmation of the doctrine of the deity of Christ.

To summarize, there is overwhelming evidence that early Christian authors, bishops, theologians, priests, and scholars vigorously proclaimed Jesus Christ our Saviour as God.

Discussion Questions:

1. What did the early writers in the Christian church believe about the deity of Christ?

2. What is the name of the heresy, which is still promoted by the Jehovah's Witnesses today, which claimed that Jesus was not God but a created being?

3. Which council of the Christian church clearly detailed what was already believed, the doctrine of the deity of Christ? In approximately what year?

4. Discuss what Clement of Rome, Ignatius, and Theophilus said about the deity of Christ.

5. Discuss what Justin Martyr and Tatian said about the deity of Christ.

6. Discuss what the Bishop of Lyons in *Refutation of Heresies* and Clement of Alexandria in *Exortation to the Greeks* both said about the deity of Christ.

7. What creed did Athanasius write and what doctrine did this creed support? Did it support the deity of Christ? Does the Trinity support the deity of Christ?

Conclusions

The goal of this research was to lay out for the reader an indisputable case for the deity of our Lord Jesus Christ. The vast majority of the evidence for the deity of Christ was drawn from the Holy Scriptures themselves. However, further support was drawn from the overwhelming consensus of early church fathers and early documents and creeds. The research began with the assumption that the Bible is the inerrant, infallible, absolute, and authoritative Word of God, and our unchangeable standard for faith and practice. Deity was defined as attesting to the fact that this Jesus of Nazareth and the personal God—the infinite, unchangeable, eternal Creator and ruler of the Universe—are one and the same and that Jesus the Christ is and was and will always be God.

This research relied on seven "streams" of evidence to support the deity of Christ. First, the straightforward claims of Jesus Christ's deity within Scripture were presented, demonstrating that the Bible clearly presents Jesus Christ as both true God and true man. The Gospel of John introduces in its first verse Jesus as God and Creator. In Hebrews 1:8 Jesus, the Son, is called God. And the incredulous Thomas, when he sees the risen Saviour cries out, "My Lord and my God."

Second, the fulfillment of dozens if not hundreds of biblical prophecies, some close to 1,000 years old, predicting things about the life and ministry Jesus should lead even the most cynical observer to submit to the conclusion that the supernatural must have been at work. There are prophecies confirming His birth, death by crucifixion, triumphal entry into Jerusalem on Palm Sunday, soldiers gambling for His clothes, even His final words on the cross. There are many other prophecies predicting with pinpoint accuracy other things in the life and ministry of Jesus. The reader is encouraged to continue to explore them and through that exploration I am certain that any suspicions will melt away.

Third, the incredibly rich use of divine names and titles which are applied to Jesus within the Word of God, ones reserved only for God Himself by commandment, were used to demonstrate that Jesus shares these names and titles with God. To name a few, in the Bible Jesus is referred to as Lord, the First and Last (eternal one), Saviour and Redeemer, the Truth and the Light, our Shepherd, and Creator.

Fourth, the words of Jesus Himself regarding His own deity makes it abundantly clear that He acknowledged Himself as God. Jesus claims He is the source of eternal life, that knowing Him is knowing God. If you have seen Him you have seen the Father. All power is given Him. We are His sheep. He is the Way, the Truth and the Life. And He gives forgiveness of sins. His gospel is truly Christ-centered. He claims that He is the "I AM," the God of Israel. His powers emanate from Him as the source, as God Himself, rather than as some intermediary.

The fifth stream of evidence painted a vivid portrait of the supernatural and divine: the birth, life, death, resurrection, and ascension of Jesus to support the case for Jesus of Nazareth's deity. He was born as no man has ever been: of a virgin, supernaturally conceived by the Holy Spirit. His life was characterized by supernatural miracles, healings, raising people from the dead, and power over the natural. His death was accompanied by supernatural events, darkness, earthquakes, rocks split in two, and graves opening. And His resurrection from the dead was witnessed by hundreds of people over a 40-day period. And the Bible lays out future prophecy yet to be fulfilled, promising His immanent return to earth to take His saints home and what will be His final eternal judgment for those who reject His offer of grace.

Sixth, a search of the biblical record was made and uncovered that in the person of Jesus Christ abides attributes identical to those of Creator God, including: holiness, omnipotence, immutability, omniscience, omnipresence, eternality, and worship. This is because they are one and the same; Jesus is God. These attributes are reserved exclusively within the Scriptures for Jehovah God and Him alone and yet they were also ascribed to Jesus Christ our Lord, which in a resounding way heralds that He is Jehovah God.

Seventh, the research clearly identified the overwhelming consensus of the early church writings and creeds that our Lord Jesus Christ is God incarnate. And the church staunchly resisted heretical attempts to challenge the deity of Christ, censoring false teaching and zealously defending this pivotal doctrine. The history of Christianity has been one in which Jesus as God was a basic assumption. And biblical Christianity was essentially characterized by the worship of the God-man Jesus Christ, the Son of God and God the Son.

There is no truth more fundamental to our faith than that of the deity of Christ. This is attested to by the fact that the early church was constantly defending this against heretical teachings denying the fact of His deity. The hope is that this small primer will be a blessing to the brothers and sisters in Christ in locking down this foundational truth, and helping them "to be ready to give an answer to every man" that Jesus was and is and ever will be very God of very God. God has left for us as Christians a clear path of breadcrumbs within Scripture to find our way from the Cross to the Throne. He has woven an intricate skein of evidence within the tapestry of His Word announcing Jesus Christ our Lord as Prophet, Priest, and King, Holy God and Saviour. Jesus Christ the King of Kings made Himself a peasant for us, to ransom us from the very fires of hell with His own agony and sacrifice. The fabric of Scripture has a beautiful skein only visible when revealed by the Holy Spirit. It is as if when we rent of our sins and trust in Jesus, God Himself spits on the ground, and makes clay of the spittle, and anoints our blind eyes so that we might see. This amazing skein, or thread, woven into the fabric of Scripture cries out incontestably, but says it so more abundantly and richly than the mere words: Jesus Christ, "My Lord and my God."

Praise His Holy Name.

Bibliography

All Scripture quotations are taken from the Holy Bible, King James Version (KJV).

Non-Web Sources:

Athanasius, (1951). *The Letters of Saint Athanasius Concerning the Holy Spirit circa 290-370: translation, introduction and notes by C.R.B. Shapland.* London, UK: Epworth Press.

Barnes, A. (1983). *Barnes' Notes on the Old and New Testaments.* Ada, MI: Baker Books.

Clarke, A. (1977). *Adam Clarke's Commentary on the Entire Bible.* Nashville, TN: Abingdon Press.

Edersheim, A. (2018). *Prophecy and History in Relation to the Messiah.* London, UK: Longmanns Green and Co.

Gill, J. (1989). *An Exposition of the Old and New Testaments: The Baptist Commentary Series.* Paris, AR: Baptist Standard Bearer.

Hanson, G. (1910). *The Resurrection and the Life*. UK: National Council of Evangelical Free Churches.

Henry, M. (1991). *Matthew Henry, Commentary on the Whole Bible*. Peabody, MA: Hendrickson Publishers.

Hodge, C. (1940). *Systematic Theology*, (1940), Volume 2. Grand Rapids, Michigan: Wm. B. Eerdsmans Publishing Co.

Josephus, F. (2013). *The Wars of the Jews, The History of the Destruction of Jerusalem*. Louisville, KY: Memoria Press.

Jurgens W. A. (Ed.) (1970). *Tatian the Syrian, Faith of Our Fathers (170 AD): Volume 1*. Sant'Anselmo, Rome: The Order of St. Benedict, Inc.

Lewis, C. S. (2015). *Mere Christianity*. San Francisco, CA: HarperOne.

Machen, J. G. (2017). *The Person of Jesus: Radio Addresses on the Deity of the Savior*. Glenside, PA: Westminister Seminary Press.

McDowell, J. & Larson, B. (1983). *Jesus, A Biblical Defense of His*

Deity. San Bernardino, CA: Here's Life Publishers, Inc.

Nee, W. (1997). *The Normal Christian Faith*. Anaheim, CA: Living Stream Ministry.

Orr, J., Nuelsen J., Mullins, E. (1994). *The International Standard Bible Encyclopedia*. Peabody, MA: Hendrickson Publishers.

Payne, J. (1980). *Encyclopedia of Biblical Prophecy: The Complete Guide to Scriptural Predictions and Their Fulfillment*. Grand Rapids, MI: Baker Book House.

Roberts, A., Donaldson, J., Coxe, A. C. (Eds.) (1994). *Hippolytus, Cyprian, Caius, Novatian: Fathers of the Third Century (The Writings of the Fathers Down to A. D. 325): Ante-Nicene Fathers, Volume 5*. Peabody, MA: Hendrickson Publishers.

Robinson, W. C. (1949), *Our Lord, An Affirmation of the Deity of Christ*. Grand Rapids, MI: Wm. B. Eerdmans Publishing Company.

Thiessen, H. C. (1949). *Introductory Lectures in Systemic Theology*.

Grand Rapids, MI: Wm. B. Eerdmans Publishing Company.

Torrey, R. A. & Dixon, A. C. (Eds.) (1994). *The Fundamentals: A Testimony to the Truth: Volume 2.* Grand Rapids, MI: Baker Book House.

Torrey, R. A. (1918). *The Fundamental Doctrines of the Christian Faith.* New York, NY: George H. Doran.

Torrey, R. A. (2004). *What the Bible Teaches: The Truths of the Bible Made Plain, Simple and Understandable.* New Kensington, PA: Whitaker House.

Walvoord, J. F. (1969). *Jesus Christ Our Lord.* Chicago, IL: Moody Press.

Warfield, B. B. (1929). *Christology and Criticism.* Oxford, UK: Oxford University Press.

Webster, N. (1967). *Webster's 1828 American Dictionary of the English Language.* Chesapeake, VA: Foundation for American Christian Education.

Web Sources:

Arnobius. (305 AD). *Against the Pagans, Vol. 1*, Retrieved April 26, 2014 from: http://www.ccel.org/ccel/schaff/anf06.xii.iii.i.xlii.html.

Athenagoras. (160 AD). *Refutation of All Heresies*, Retrieved April 26, 2014 from: http://www.clerus.org/pls/clerus/cn_clerus.h_centro?dicastero=2&tema=7&argomento=25&sottoargomento=88&lingua=2&classe=1&operazione=ges_formaz&vers=3&rif=65&rif1=65.

Clement of Alexandria. (190 AD). *Exhortation to the Greeks*, Retrieved April 26, 2014 from: http://archive.org/stream/clementofalexand00clem/clementof alexand00clem_djvu.txt.

Clement of Rome. (Circa 92-99 AD). *2nd Epistle of Clement to the Corinthians*, Retrieved April 26, 2014 from: http://carm.org/second-epistle-of-clement-to-the-corinthians.

First Council of Nicea. (Circa 325 AD). *The Nicene Creed*,

Retrieved September 19, 2021 from:
https://www.ccel.org/creeds/nicene.creed.html.

Ignatius, Bishop of Antioch. (Circa 110 AD). *Epistle of Ignatius to the Ephesians*. Retrieved April 26, 2014 from: http://www.sacred-texts.com/bib/lbob/lbob18.htm http://www.sacred-texts.com/bib/lbob/lbob20.htm http://www.sacredtexts.com/bib/lbob/lbob21.htm.

Iranaeus. (Circa 200 AD). *Irenaeus Against Heresies: book 1 and 3*, Retrieved April 26, 2014 from: http://www.ccel.org/ccel/schaff/anf01.ix.iv.xx.html http://www.ccel.org/ccel/schaff/anf01.ix.ii.xi.html.

Justin Martyr. (140 AD). *Dialogue with Tropho*, Retrieved April 26, 2014 from: www.earlychristianwritings.com/text/justinmartyr-dialoguetrypho.html.

Mathetes. (Unknown, 130 AD-third century), *Epistle of Mathetes to Diognetus*, Retrieved April 26, 2014 from: http://www.ccel.org/ccel/schaff/anf01.iii.ii.vii.html.

Melito of Sardis. (177 AD). *Fragment in Anastasius of Sinai's: The Guide 13*, Retrieved April 26, 2014 from: http://www.earlychristianwritings.com/text/melito.html.

Novatian. (235 AD). *Treatise on the Trinity*, Retrieved April 26, 2014 from: http://www.ccel.org/ccel/schaff/anf05.vi.iii.xii.html.

Tertullian. (Circa 215 AD). *The Flesh of Christ*, Retrieved April 26, 2014 from: http://www.ccel.org/ccel/schaff/anf03.v.vii.v.html http://www.ccel.org/ccel/schaff/anf03.v.ix.xiii.html http://biblehub.com/library/tertullian/a_treatise_on _the_soul/.

Theophilus. (Circa 160 AD). *Bishop of Antioch To Autolycus.* Retrieved April 26, 2014 from: http://www.ccel.org/ccel/schaff/anf02.iv.ii.ii.xxii.html.

Bibliography

Appendix

Table 1: Prophecies of the Messiah Fulfilled

Prophecy	Fulfillment
That Jesus will be the mighty God; Isaiah 9:6	John 1:1, 14 Hebrews 1:8
That He will be raised from the dead; Psalms 16:10, 30:3; Matthew 20:18-19	Matthew 28:1-10 John 20:11-31 1 Corinthians 15:3-8
Messiah to be sold for 30 pieces of silver; Zechariah 11:12	Matthew 26:15
Tortured by whipping; Isaiah 50:6, 53:5	Matthew 27:26, 29 Mark 15:15 John 19:1
From the line of David; 2 Samuel 7:12; Isaiah 9:6-7, 11:1-5	Matthew 1:1 Romans 1:3 Acts 2:30
His final words on the cross; Psalm 22:1	Matthew 27:46 Mark 15:34
Buried in rich man's tomb; Isaiah 53:9	Matthew 27:57-60

Jesus would be spit on; Isaiah 50:6	Matthew 27:30
Messenger will prepare the way; Malachi 3:1	Mark 1:1-4 John 1:6-7
Bones out of joint; Psalm 22:14	Implied by crucifixion
His visage marred more than any man; Isaiah 52:14	Matthew 27:26, 29-30 Mark 14:65, 15:15, 19 John 19:1-3
Betrayed for 30 pieces of silver; Zechariah 11:12-13	Matthew 26:14-15, 27:3-10
Jesus' disciples would forsake Him and flee; Zechariah 13:6-7	Matthew 26:56 Mark 14:50
He will heal the blind, deaf, dumb, and lame; Isaiah 35:5-6	Matthew 9:30, 11:5, 15:30-31 Mark 7:31
God will call his "child" from Egypt; Hosea 11:1	Matthew 2:13-15

www.ingramcontent.com/pod-product-compliance
Lightning Source LLC
Chambersburg PA
CBHW070439130626
46553CB00006B/2257